Bibbity Boozity Book

Guy Hutchinson

Table of Contents

ACKNOWLEDGEMENTS

This book would not be possible without the following people. Of course Walt Disney famously said "It's kind of fun to do the impossible."

So Walt would have done this book without the following people, and he would have had fun doing it.

Actually, the full quote from Walt Disney was "Write this down: it's kind of fun to do the impossible, like licking your elbow or reading a book with your eyes closed. Totally fun to do and totally impossible. Nah, scratch that last part. Is this my drink or yours? I thought mine had ice."

Anyway, these people were helpful to me:

Dana Snyder - My co-host from Drunk On Disney and my dear friend, he has paid for more than his share of rounds at Disney bars.

Bart Scott – For being an inspirational friend.

Jon Eadler – Because if I mention his name he'll probably buy a copy.

My Aunt Judy – Because she'd buy three copies even if I don't mention her.

You – For still reading this. I imagine most have skipped ahead. I was going to use this space to store my passwords. Oh well. Thanks, you.

INTRO

Hey there.

Here you are holding this book. Maybe you got it as a gift. Perhaps you bought it yourself. Maybe you found it discarded on the men's room floor.

Regardless, I am in your hands. That puts you in my hands as well. I am going to guide you through the Walt Disney World Resort with my very capable hands. I'll hold your hand.

Trust me. I have nice hands. I use moisturizer and everything.
Walt Disney World is a paradise for cocktail lovers. It's supposed to be. The people that made it must have been drunk. How else can you account for Goofy? He's a dog and Pluto's a dog. The difference? Pluto was designed in the morning and Goofy was designed after a 3 martini lunch.

Think about it.

Every single day thousands of parents enter into a Disney park to stand in long lines, sweat in the hot sun and spend away their life's saving. How do those parents leave happy? Because when you are choking down a yard of Bass Ale outside a red phone booth in the UK Pavilion or drinking some crazy Disney created cocktail outside Spaceship Earth all of that stress leaves your body. It's science.

Now, if this book was only useful at the theme park you would only get to break it out once a year or so. That's why this book has another purpose.

You can use it at home.

Since we started *Drunk On Disney* back in 2013 I have been fascinated with bringing the taste of Disney home. Here in this book you will find my versions of the delicious (and/or) wacky Disney cocktails.

Figuring out these drink recipes isn't really easy. Disney generally lists all of the ingredients on the menu, but it's a bit of juggling to find the right combination and proper amounts to get the drink right.

Over many years and many Disney trips I have bought gallons of Disney concoctions and then, days later tried to recreate them. Often the recipe I give you isn't exact, but it evokes the same taste. Sometimes I had to replace ingredients or add something new to replace the Disney magic that was missing. In the end, I'm really happy with these drinks and I think you will love them.

I care about you. I love you. Remember when I talked about holding your hand? I am going to hold your hand even after both our hands get sweaty and gross. Figuratively. But the point is, "this is the beginning of a beautiful friendship."

Guy's notes: The line "this is the beginning of a beautiful friendship" comes from the Casablanca scene in The Great Movie Ride. The animatronic Humphrey Bogart says it to the animatronic Claude Rains before they hop inside the plane… which is the actual real plane from the movie. 100% true... I think… That ride is gone so you can't check it.

Walt Liked Booze

Do you feel a little strange downing shots of tequila in the Mexico Pavilion when you can hear Donald Duck crooning tunes from The Three Caballeros? Don't. Walt wouldn't want you to feel strange.

If Walt was alive he would look at you, take a long drag on a Chesterfield, give a little chuckle and flash a warm smile and say "I only hope you never lose sight of one thing - my sexy mustache." Then he would pound a shot of tequila and start telling you stories about hopping on a moving train with Ward Kimball on a warm night in Mexico after having one too many shots. Then he'd put you in a headlock and start giving you a noogie and you'd say "Walt! Act your age!" He'd realize he's about 127 years old and he'd turn into a pile of dust.

We all love Walt. We revere him. He was about two things: having fun and making sure others had fun. He didn't create every character or every ride, but he created the environment where they could be created.

And he liked booze.

Walt famously enjoyed a Scotch Mist at the end of every day at the studio. His secretary, Tommie Wilck, would make it and said she watered it down. They serve a Scotch Mist at the Carthay Circle Lounge in Disney's California Adventure in Anaheim. They use Black and White Scotch. People say it was Walt's favorite brand and that seems to make sense. It has two little Scotty dogs (one black and one white) frolicking on the label. It seems like the type of bottle the man who produced Lady and the Tramp would buy.

Walt wasn't the only one that liked booze. Mickey Mouse has been known sample the occasional cocktail. In the 1928 short "Galloping Gaucho" the mouse drinks beer, smokes cigarettes, chews tobacco and kills a drifter (scene deleted.)

Guy's notes: Below are some of the favorite liquors of classic Disney characters.

Mickey Mouse: Heavy is the head of the king, so he needs a stiff drink. Mickey likes whiskey. But he is a cartoon mouse so he tosses a jar of maraschino cherries in each glass.

Minnie Mouse: Fruity flavored martinis.

Donald Duck: Donald is a mean drunk. He likes gin with a gin chaser.

Tinkerbell: A thimbleful of whatever you have.

R2D2: Axle grease and rum, cut with a splash of soda.

Don Knotts: Peppermint Schnapps

Walt Disney didn't mind having characters drink or get drunk! Remember Dumbo? There is a scene where the clowns have a champagne toast and the champagne ends up being guzzled down by Dumbo and Timothy. This leads to the iconic pink elephant drunken sequence.
Walt even wanted the Dumbo attraction to be a series of pink elephants that guests would ride on.

Enjoy your Disney drinking. It's what Walt would do.

Magic Kingdom

When I started working on this book (in 2014) Magic Kingdom was a dry park. I don't mean that literally, because it rains about every 35 minutes in Orlando.
But Magic Kingdom didn't serve drinks until Be Our Guest opened in 2018. Here's what I wrote back then:

The Magic Kingdom was the first of Disney's Florida theme parks and it's the one everyone always thinks of when they think of Walt Disney World.

Entering the park we walk past a series of turn of the century series of shops. They all sell stuffed animals. That's probably not authentic. When I think of old timey streets I think of gentlemen with huge mustaches drinking pint after pint from a publican who only cleans the glass by wiping it down with a filthy rag. But Disney doesn't serve any beer here. They once had functioning tobacco shop where you could get a fat cigar and puff away like some kind of robber baron. But even that is gone. You can buy a Mickey Mouse plush and hug it like some kind of robber baron.

Note: I don't know what a robber baron is.

Keep going and we get to the castle. Now, historically castles had the best booze but there is no booze to be had here.

Magic Kingdom is designed to be a "hub and spoke." This means that the castle is the center of the wheel and the other lands jut out of the center of the wheel.

Frontierland is evocative of the old west! They had tons of booze back then! You should be able to knock back a whiskey in the saloon, but you can't. No booze here. Move on.

Adventureland is evocative of the old jungle. Or new jungle. Not sure. Wherever it is, I think they have booze there. They use it to sterilize snake bites. But alas, no booze here. Move on.

Liberty Square is supposed to be during the revolutionary war era. Serious boozing going on. Otherwise how could you explain how ridiculous Abe Lincoln looks? Actually I know Lincoln wasn't born at that time. So don't send me letters about that. But do send me letters! I get awfully lonely. Regardless, no booze.

This park never had any booze until they expanded Fantasyland and opened the Be Our Guest Restaurant. There you can drink wine and champagne from France.

The only land with booze is Fantasyland which should probably be the one without booze. The whole thing is backwards.

Note: I skipped Tomorrowland because I don't wanna imagine a future without booze.

My, how things have changed. My writing has gotten so much worse and now I know what a robber baron is.

Now, virtually every sit down restaurant at Magic Kingdom serves some kind of alcoholic beverages.

That said, there aren't that many great cocktails in Magic Kingdom. This isn't to say there aren't good things to drink, there certainly are. Fess Parker's wine is available all over Magic Kingdom and I have a rule that I always buy booze when it's named after a dead celebrity and Fess is a great one. He played Davey Crockett in the legendary Disney series.

Guy's notes: Guy wanted you to know Fess was also the dad in *Old Yeller*. Also, Guy isn't sure why Guy is interrupting Guy to give notes.

There's some other fun drinks to be had in Magic Kingdom. Over in *Liberty Tree Tavern* they serve a "Warm Washington Cider" which is a Washington brand hard cider served warm and topped with baker's crème.

The drink from Magic Kingdom is a pretty simple shandy, but it's got a great toast. Enjoy!

Schweitzer's Shandy

Compare to 'Jungle Navigation Co. Shandy' at Jungle Navigation Co. LTD Skipper Canteen at Magic Kingdom.

4 oz Blue Moon Belgian White Ale
4 oz Simply Lemonade

Mix the cold Simply Lemonade (brand of lemonade) with the Blue Moon Belgian White Ale in a beer glass and serve.

A Toast to Albert Schweitzer

Albert Schweitzer is the butt of a joke we all know, but we probably don't all really get. On the Jungle Cruise most tours contain the joke that waterfall is named Schweitzer Falls after Dr. Albert Falls.

When the Jungle Cruise opened in 1955 Schweitzer was very well known. Three years prior he had been awarded the Nobel Peace Prize for his, rather simple, philosophy "Reverence for Life" which said that "...good consists in maintaining, assisting and enhancing life, and to destroy, to harm or to hinder life is evil." Schweitzer received his medical degree

in 1912 and worked at his own expense in Africa. He then founded the Albert Schweitzer Hospital.
For all his good work and for sorta giving his name to the falls, we salute Dr. Albert... Schweitzer.

Guy's notes: Wikipedia says Schweitzer was an "Alsatian polymath" which I was pretty sure was a Decepticon. However, clicking the words showed the definition. Alsatian is a region in France and a polymath as "an individual whose knowledge spans a significant number of subjects, known to draw on complex bodies of knowledge to solve specific problems."
Albert Schweitzer knew a lot of stuff. He wrote books on Jesus Christ and Paul the Apostle. He studied medicine and was a music scholar. Now, when I hear the 'Albert Falls' joke I will truly get the reference.

EPCOT Center

Ok, here's where things get serious. For starters, I know they don't put EPCOT in all caps anymore, but I do because I want you to imagine me yelling "EPCOT" at you all the time. Also, I know it's not called EPCOT Center anymore, but I'm not giving that one up. The park was originally called EPCOT Center and then in 1994 they dropped the Center and started calling the park "Epcot '94" which seemed weird until you drank so much sake in the Japan Pavilion that you couldn't remember what year it was. Then it really came in handy.

EPCOT Center is really a wonderful place to go cocktail sampling. The World Showcase half of the park allows you to feel like you are travelling all around the world, assuming you don't know world geography very well.

Because of World Showcase many people like to challenge themselves to 'Drink Around the World.' To do this you have to walk around EPCOT Center trying a drink in each country. When you finish, you'll probably be hammered. You'll have also spent $186 on drinks. I suggest you just drink any 11 cocktails from this book and just read the toast to each in a different offensive accent.

Berusetfjell

Compare to 'Fjellbekk' at Akershus
Royal Banquet Hall at Norway
Pavilion at EPCOT Center.

1 oz Aquavit
1 oz Vikingfjord Vodka
4 oz Sprite
1 oz Lime Juice

Stir Aquavit, vodka and lime juice in
a highball glass and slowly add the
Sprite. Garnish with a lime wedge and
a sprig of spruce.

A Toast to Olav V of Norway

Olav served as the King of Norway
from 1957 until his death in 1991.
Olav was known as the "People's
King," and was extremely popular.
He loved to ski and on boarded a
suburban train in his skiing outfit.
When asked about his safety concerns
travelling on public transport he
said he had "4 million bodyguards"
referring to the total population of
Norway.

Olav was the biggest supporter of the concept that became the Norway Pavilion in EPCOT Center.
As the Vikings did, let's raise a glass and say "skål!" as we drink to Olav V!

Guy's notes: The name of the drink in EPCOT is 'Fjellbekk' with "fjell" meaning "mountain" and "bekk" meaning "stream."
Our version is called Berusetfjell with the word for "drunk" replacing stream. I can't imagine the translation makes sense, but a drunk mountain is probably the most Norwegian thing ever.
Garnishes are always optional, but really make the drink more visually appealing which does make you think it tastes better. Of course, once you get to your third or fourth one just garnish the drink with your mouth.

Boisson des France

Compare to 'Cocktail des Chefs' at Les Chefs de France at France Pavilion at EPCOT Center.

3 oz Champagne
1 oz Lejay cassis

Pour Lejay in champagne flute and top with champagne.

A Toast to Gaston Lenôtre

Gaston was a famous French chef. He is considered to be the creator of a popular French dessert known as the 'opera cake.' He founded a culinary empire creating cooking schools, restaurants and a vast catering service.
In 1982 he worked with Paul Bocuse and Roger Vergé to create a restaurant in the new EPCOT Center. The restaurant's name referred to the three creators, Les Chefs de France. Let's raise our glass high and say "À votre santé!"

Guy's notes: Gaston was also used as part the inspiration of Chef Gusteau in the movie *Ratatouille*.

Disney lists this as Lejay and "sparkling wine" on the menu. The difference between sparkling wine and champagne is that champagne IS sparkling wine that comes from the region of Champagne, France. If it is not from that area it is just called sparkling wine.
I prefer to use actual champagne since it's a true French cocktail.
Lejay Cassis is a liqueur made from the berry of the Blackcurrant shrub. Lejay was made from a partnership between Auguste-Denis Lagoute and Henri Lejay in the 1840s. It is an excellent liqueur that is a fine addition to your liquor cabinet. I would recommend trying some straight after you enjoy this cocktail.

Boozie Frappe

Compare to 'Matcha Frappe' at Teppan Edo at Japan Pavilion at EPCOT Center.

1 oz Rum
1 oz Sake
4 oz Condensed Milk
1 oz Amoretti Green Tea Syrup
2 drops Green food coloring

Mix condensed milk and green tea syrup with 2 cups ice in a blender on low slowly increasing to high. Pour into hurricane glass and stir in rum, sake and a couple drops of green food coloring. Don't stir thoroughly, leave some separation between the white and the green.

A Toast to Jack Boyd

Jack was a multitalented Disney worker who worked as an animator for several decades. His animation work covers everything from *Cinderella* to *Condorman*. That being noted, it is his single writing and single directing credit that made the strongest impact on Disney park guests.
Jack wrote the script for the Disneyland film *The Walt Disney*

Story which had a run on Main Street U.S.A. in both Disneyland and Magic Kingdom.
His sole directing credit was for the EPCOT attraction Universe of Energy. Friends, muster up all of the energy you can to salute Jack Boyd!

Guy's notes: This is an interesting drink. If you don't want to invest in a bottle of green tea syrup for this you can try it with simple syrup. Or you can substitute amaretto for an Italian twist.
Teppan Edo is a Teppanyaki restaurant where the food is cooked right at your table on an iron griddle table top. These are commonly referred to as "hibachi" restaurants, although true hibachi is cooked on a grill with and open grate.
The name Teppan Edo is a combination of Teppanyaki and Edo which is the Japanese name for a time period between 1603 and 1868. At that time Edo was the name of what is modern Tokyo.

Crown Prince's Cup

Compare to 'Prince of Norway' at Akershus Royal Banquet Hall at Norway Pavilion at EPCOT Center.

1 oz Apricot Brandy
1 oz Hofland Sloe Gin
1 oz sour mix
2 oz orange Juice

Combine Apricot Brandy, Sloe Gin and sour mix in a cocktail shaker with ice and shake lightly. Strain and pour into a red wine glass. Top with orange juice but don't stir.

A Toast to Princess Märtha of Sweden

The Crown Prince's Cup is a rather delicate drink and is named after Harald V of Norway. Harald V visited EPCOT, as Crown Prince, in 1988 to dedicate the pavilion.

It is fitting to raise a toast to his mother, Princess Märtha of Sweden. In addition to being the mother of Harald (who is currently King) but also the wife of Olav V, but alas she died of cancer before her husband ascended to the throne. The Swedish layer cake, Princess Cake, was named after her and her sisters. Let us raise the cup named for her son and raise our voices to Princess Märtha!

Guy's notes: Sloe gin is a liquor made from gin and sloe which is a type of drupe. A drupe is a term that is a bit confusing because it includes a wide variety of ordinary foods that seemingly don't have much in common. These include coffee, mango, cashews and coconuts.
The sloe looks a lot like a blueberry. Sloe gin is tart and full of flavor. I recommend you have a shot on the side to fully get the flavor.

Goka Gust

Compare to 'Japanese Breeze' at Teppan Edo at Japan Pavilion at EPCOT Center.

1 oz Coconut Rum
5 oz Lakewood PURE Cranberry Juice
3 oz Goya Pineapple Juice

Fill a tulip glass with ice and pour rum over top. Mix the cranberry and pineapple well and add to glass. Top with orange wedge.

A Toast to Mitsui Takatoshi

In the 1600s Mitsui Takatoski opened multiple clothing stores and textile shops. His work later led to the
Mitsukoshi retail shopping chain. The chain has dozens of locations including one at the Japan Pavilion in EPCOT Center.
It is with gratitude for the countless hours we have spent watching oysters sliced open as we shopped for shrimp flavored pixie

sticks and weird plus dolls of cat buses. Mitsui, this one's for you! Kampai!

Guy's notes: With this drink we remember the man who brought us the weirdest store on Disney property as well as the village of Goka. It was merged with 3 other villages and towns to create the town of Okinoshima in 2004. Lakewood PURE Cranberry Juice is great in this because it's got a very tart taste that works so well in this one. If you can't find it, just look for one with as little added sugar as possible. The pineapple juice will sugar it up plenty. "Kampai" is a traditional Sake toast. It literally means "dry cup" which makes a whole lot of sense to me!

Lightning in a Glass

Compare to 'Raju' at
Takumi-Tei at Japan Pavilion at
EPCOT Center.

2 oz Haku Japanese Vodka
6 oz Spiced Ginger Beer
1 oz Lime juice

Pour ginger beer into pint glass and stir in vodka and lime juice.

A Toast to King Mohammed V

When the King of Morocco was scheduled to visit the United States in 1957 he had a specific request, he wanted to see Disneyland. Walt Disney, never missing a chance to generate publicity for the park, met the ruler at the park and gave him a four hour guided tour. The Moroccan King is seen, in traditional garb, smiling alongside Walt as he rode a Storybookland Canal Boat and enjoyed the views of the park.

Legend has it that after the King retreated to his hotel room he instructed his aides to change into "American style" clothing. They did, and so did the monarch. Now, incognito, they returned to the park where the king purchased tickets and continued to ride on the thrills of Disneyland. When spotted by a Disney executive, Mohammed

reportedly said that he wanted to experience the park as a regular guest because he thought that looked like more fun than the guided tour with reporters. To a true Disney fan! Long live the King!

Guy's notes: The EPCOT version is called Raju after the legendary thunder beast from Japanese Mythology. This drink does have a bit of a kick with a ginger beer base. Haku is a quality vodka distilled from Japanese white rice. You can substitute Haku, but only if you get permission from Bobby Heenan. Sorry, that's a bad wrestling joke. Seriously, you can substitute Haku, but try and get a Japanese rice vodka like AO Vodka.

Medigan

Compare to 'Americano' at Via Napoli Ristorante e Pizzeria at Italy Pavilion at EPCOT Center.

1.5 oz Campari
1 oz Sweet vermouth
4 oz Perrier

Pour Campari and sweet vermouth into an old fashioned glass filled with ice. Top with Perrier and garnish with a lemon wheel.

A Toast to Robert Jani

Robert Jani produced large scale spectacular events. He produced the "Honor America Day" in Washington D.C. for the Nixon administration. He also produced Super Bowl half time shows and reimagined the Radio City Music Hall stage show.
In the 1960s he produced and created parades for the Disney Company, most notably The Main Street Electrical Parade. Jani has been honored with a dedicated window on Main Street in Disneyland, and we honor him with this toast! To Robert Jani!

Guy's notes: This is simply an Americano. Medigan was how my Italian grandmother pronounced "American" and it seems like a perfect name.
The Americano was invented by Gaspare Campari in the 1860s.
The Americano is ordered by James Bond in more than one of Ian Fleming's stories. In "From a View to a Kill" Bond stipulates that the drink should be made with Perrier so that's how we made it.

After all, who am I to argue with James Bond?

Reef-a-Rita

Compare to 'Coral 'Rita' at
Coral Reef Restaurant at EPCOT Center.

1.5 oz Patrón Añejo Tequila
1 oz Triple sec
1 oz Lime juice

Mix Patron, triple sec and lime juice
in a shaker, shake and pour into a
salt rimmed cosmo glass. Garnish with
a lime wedge.

A Toast to Burton Sperber

Burton Sperber was the founder of the
ValleyCrest Landscape Companies. He
founded the company in 1949 when he
was just 19 years old. For over 60
years ValleyCrest was the landscape
company to turn to for spectacular
design and presentation. ValleyCrest
designed landscaping for zoos, hotels
and highways around the world. In the
mid-1990s it was Burton and
ValleyCrest that Disney turned to when
they needed to turn Florida swampland
into an African Savanah for Animal
Kingdom (which is the largest theme

park in the world.) In addition to
running a landscaping empire, Burton
was a master magician with the largest
collection of magic books in the
world. For a man who brought a little
more magic to the world, to Burton!

Guy's notes: Burton Sperber's
daughter, Wendie Jo Sperber was an
accomplished actress who appeared in
dozens of movies and TV shows. Her
most famous role was as Marty McFly's
sister in *Back to the Future.* She also
had a funny turn in an episode of the
Disney sitcom *Dinosaurs* where she
played the daughter of B.P. Richfield
and was rumored to eat the boys she
dated.

Sarah's Apple

Compare to 'Ottawa Apple' at Le Cellier Steakhouse at Canada Pavilion at EPCOT Center.

2 oz Crown Apple Maple Whisky
2 oz Cranberry Juice
1 apple (for infusing with whisky)

Infuse this whisky with an apple. To do this, slice an apple and put in a mason jar. Fill jar with whisky and store in a dark place for 5 days and then strain.

To mix drink, add cold cranberry juice to an old fashioned glass with ice. Stir in whiskey and garnish with apple slice.

A Toast to Jean Shepherd

When visitors sit in the rotating theater to watch the Carousel of Progress for the first time, a cool feeling comes upon them.
Partially it's the cool of air conditioning after stepping out of the Florida sun. But there's another feeling and it's a tugging of nostalgia for Christmases of the past.

Now, the Carousel is all about nostalgia (and of course Progress) but the distinctive voice of Shepherd reminds viewers of his narration on *A Christmas Story*. To

a brilliant storyteller! To Jean Shepard!

Guy's notes: The Carousel of Progress is a ride. It's also a show. First and foremost, it's a ride.
If King Arthur's Carousel is a ride, so is this.
There are some other familiar voices in the Carousel of Progress. The current cast includes B.J. Ward (Velma from *Scooby Doo,*) Debi Derryberry (*Jimmy Neutron*) and Janet Waldo (*Josie and the Pussycats*) not to mention Mel Blanc shouting "No Privacy at all around this place!"
There's much more to Jean Shepherd's career than *A Christmas Story* and Carousel of Progress. His radio show lasted for decades and his stories are wonderful and easy to be found online.

The Stave

Compare to 'The Stavanger' at Akershus Royal Banquet Hall at Norway Pavilion at EPCOT Center.

2 oz Welch's Strawberry Raspberry juice
1 oz Vikingfjord Vodka
1 oz Linie Aquavit

Shake ingredients in a shaker full of ice. Pout into cosmo glass and garnish with 2 raspberries.

A Toast to Morgan Evans

Walt Disney loved railroads and decided to build a miniature railroad in his backyard which he called the 'Carolwood Pacific Railroad.' Walt hired Morgan and his brother Jack to design a landscape for the railroad. Walt continued to employ Morgan doing landscaping on an even bigger scale at Disneyland. When Walt saw topiaries in Europe he returned and told Morgan to replicate them. After two years of work, Morgan introduced topiaries to Disney parks and they have been a staple ever since. To Morgan Evans for making the world more fun to look at!

Guy's notes: The Norway Pavilion uses Vikingfjord vodka, but I noticed they don't always use it in this drink. You should request it when you are there, but you can substitute any other vodka unless you have some on hand.
Linie is a potato based spirit that is given a secret blend of Nordic herbs and then sent on a ship around the world to mature.
It's a pretty great liquor.
Disney calls this drink 'The Stavenger' after the Norwegian city.
I changed the name to 'The Stave' as a reference to The Stave Church building at the front of the pavilion. Stave Churches are so named because the type of lumber is called 'stav' in Norwegian.

Disney's Hollywood Studios

This is probably my least favorite of all the Florida Disney parks. Still, its setting provides some great drinking atmosphere.

The golden age of Hollywood and the concept of television and movie making (and television and movie watching) has led to the immersive environments here.

You can go to Sci-Fi Dine-In Theater and enjoy a cocktail in the seat of a vintage car. Or soak in the vibes at The Hollywood Brown Derby.

This park is also unique because of the leftover influences from the Disney-MGM Studios days. Today it seems less likely that a new Disney park would ever be built with so many references to movies and shows that Disney doesn't have ownership of.

Disney's Hollywood Studios is currently divided into different areas, many of which are inspired by neighborhoods in Hollywood and Los Angeles, California. Hollywood Boulevard, Echo Lake, Grand Avenue and Sunset Boulevard all have roots in real places in California.

It's also home to Gertie the Dinosaur, one of the best Disney theme park dinosaur sculptures. Gertie used to be lower on the list before they closed Ellen's Energy Adventure. Now the only existing giant dinosaur sculptures are the dozens of dinosaur sculptures at Animal Kingdom. Also outside the T-Rex restaurant. Plus, possibly that weird Lego sea dragon. Maybe that's supposed to be a dinosaur. I guess you can also count the dinosaur float in the Electric Water Pageant. What's with all the dinosaurs, Disney?!?

I found the cocktails in this chapter to be really delightful. Once I told people that I enjoyed a bottle of Colt 45 because it reminded me of hot dogs. These facts may be unrelated.

The Divine Margarita

Compare to 'Patrón Platinum Margarita'
at Tune-In Lounge at Disney's
Hollywood Studios.

2 oz Patrón Silver Tequila
1 oz Cointreau
2 oz Lime Juice
3 oz Sweet-and-Sour

Salt the rim of a welled margarita
glass and mix the ingredients in a
shaker. Pour over ice.

A Toast to Walter Parr

Reverend Walter Parr was a preacher
born in Liverpool, England. He
journeyed to America in the late 1800s
to attend seminary in Chicago. After
seminary he stayed in Illinois and was
ordained Congregational ministry in
Clifton.
It was here that he became friends
with Elias Disney who named his
youngest son Walt, after the Reverend.
Without Reverend Walter Parr there
wouldn't be a WDW. There might be a
BDW or a JDW or a SDW or something
else. So to WDW and Walter Parr we say
Cheers and God Bless!

Guy's notes: It's interesting to think of how things would be different if Walt wasn't named Walt. There have been many famous Walters over the years, Walter Mondale, Walter Matthau, Walter Payton and some famous Walts, particularly poet Walt Whitman. But, it's Walt Disney that I imagine most people think of when they hear the name Walt.

This drink is a pretty classic margarita and is perfect with Patrón Silver Tequila.

The Tune-In Lounge is a really cool bar that is covered with vintage televisions and has a wonderfully quirky 1950's vibe. It's part of the 50's Prime Time Café so it's great to check out if you'd like to eat there but have other dining plans.

Fire and Cream

Compare to 'Fireball Cocktail' at 50's Prime Time Café at Disney's Hollywood Studios.

1.5 oz Fireball Whisky
1.5 oz RumChata Cream Liqueur

Fill a rocks glass with ice, add both liquors and stir.

A Toast to Oliver Wallace

Oliver Wallace was a London born composer who made music for many Disney films including Dumbo, Peter Pan and Cinderella.
His long list of musical credits is dotted with a very few voice acting roles, the first of which was as Winkie the bartender in *The Adventures of Ichabod and Mr. Toad*. Winkie is immortalized spinning drinks behind the bar in the Disneyland ride Mr. Toad's Wild Ride. To the voice of one of the few characters to tend bar inside of a Disney ride, we raise a glass to Oliver Wallace!

Guy's notes: This is as simple as it gets. Two ingredients in a glass with ice.

Fireball and RumChata have quickly become popular in the USA, with the proof being the number of airplane bottles of both you see on the ground along the freeway.

Fireball has a backstory that feels like something from Disney Imagineering. Originally it was marketed as "Dr. McGillicuddy's Fireball Whisky" after the absurdly named mascot Dr. Aloysius Percival McGillicuddy who was a bartender in the old west.

RumChata comes in a weird bottle that looks a bit more like a bottle of shampoo than liquor. The name comes from a combination of Rum and horchata (which is a catchall name for various types of plant based milks.)

This drink is served outside of Disney at various college bars under the name "Cinnamon Toast Crunch shot."

Hard Cold Brew

Compare to 'Cold Brew XO' at 50's Prime Time Café at Disney's Hollywood Studios.

2 oz Patrón XO Café Coffee Liqueur
1 oz Heavy Cream
3 oz Cold Brew

Make your cold brew the night before. Add ingredients to an Irish coffee mug and stir. Top with ice.

A Toast to Simeon Skillin

Simeon Skillin was the very first American sculptor, born in 1747. Born in Boston, Simeon and his sons were known for their fine artistry in wooden sculptures of Native American men. Because of the general illiteracy of the era, symbols were commonly used outside stores to indicate what was sold inside. The striped pole indicated haircuts, the winding snakes symbolized medicine and the 'wooden Indian' told passersby that cigars and other tobacco products could be found inside.
For decades customers on Main Street in Disneyland and WDW's Magic Kingdom

could find tobacco products in a shop behind a wooden Indian named Chief Seegar. Seegar (and his counterpart in front of the Westward Ho Trading Co. in Frontierland) still adorn the streets in Disney parks as a reminder of the past and craftsmen like Simeon Skillin. So let's raise our brew to Simeon!

Guy's notes: This is a very pleasant coffee drink. If you're a big coffee fan you can double or triple the coffee and serve it in a pint glass.
Disney actually serves this in an Old Fashioned glass, but probably more out of convenience. It works better in an Irish coffee mug or just your favorite coffee mug.
The 50's Prime Time Café is one of the most fun venues at Disney's Hollywood Studios if you're up for it. The gag is that the waitress/waiter will pretend to be a pushy relative making sure you finish your vegetables and stuff some crackers in your purse for later.
If you have young children it's fun for them to see mom and dad "put in their place."

I Can't Believe it's Not Windex!

Compare to 'Dad's Electric Lemonade' at Tune-In Lounge at Disney's Hollywood Studios.

1 and 1/2 oz Vodka
1/2 oz Blue Curaçao
2 oz Sweet-and-Sour
1 oz Sprite

Mix your vodka, sweet and sour and Blue Curaçao in a shaker with ice. Pour out into plastic cup and top with Sprite.

A Toast to Thelma Howard

In 1951 Thelma Howard started a job tending house for Walt and Lillian Disney. Thelma took care of the house and the family for decades and treasured her many fond memories with the Disneys. When she passed away at a Santa Monica nursing home it was discovered that she had gotten more than memories from her time at the Disney household.
Walt had gifted Thelma with a gift of stock every Christmas that she worked

for him. She never cashed out and at the time of her death her stock was worth over 9 million dollars. She left half to her son and half to a charity

to benefit homeless children. To Thelma!

Guy's notes: Disney puts a light up ice cube in this. They are available for sale online or you can bring one home from your previous trip and re-use it when you make your own brew. It works really well with the blue drink and makes it look electric!
You can always substitute Triple Sec for Blue Curaçao (and vice versa.)
The difference is just the blue coloring and Triple Sec tends to have a higher alcohol content.
Curaçao is a liquor made from the peel of a bitter orange. It's actually naturally colorless, but the blue is added to make dynamic cocktails like this.

Ken Berry Lemonade

Compare to 'Very Berry Lemonade' at Catalina Eddies at Disney's Hollywood Studios.

2 oz Bacardi Superior Rum,
4 oz odwalla® Lemonade
4 oz Strawberry Purée

Mix lemonade and purée in a blender with 6 ice cubes. Blend until smooth and add to glass. Add rum and stir. Garnish with a lime wedge.

A Toast to Ken Berry

Ken was a friendly face on TV screens in the 1960s, 1970s and 1980s appearing on *F Troop*, *The Carol Burnett Show* and *Mama's Family*.
After he graduated high school Berry volunteered for the Army and served under Sergeant Leonard Nimoy (later of Star Trek fame) who encouraged him to pursue a career in entertainment.
Disney fans will undoubtedly recall his performances in *The Cat From Outer Space* and *Herbie Rides Again*.
Let us raise our glass to, the one and only, Ken Berry!

Guy's notes: Disney serves this one in a plastic cup which isn't a bad way to go. This is a great summer cocktail. Imagine the Florida sun beating down on you as you stand in line for this beverage eyeballing the ever growing line for *Tower of Terror*.

Then laugh because you're on your couch watching *Herbie Rides Again* and sippin' a Ken Berry Lemonade.

This recipe calls for odwalla® Lemonade which is billed as all-natural. If you can't find some, look for a bottled lemonade that's not too sugary because the strawberry purée usually has lots of sugar in it.

You can make the strawberry purée yourself by washing and hulling a batch of strawberries and then sticking them in your blender. You can also buy it in a bottle. But you should make it yourself and make fresh lemonade. Do it. Do it for Ken Berry.

Louella's Martini

Compare to 'Grapefruit Cake Martini' at The Hollywood Brown Derby at Disney's Hollywood Studios.

1.5 oz Deep Eddy Ruby Red Grapefruit Vodka
1.5 oz Stoli Vanil Vodka
a splash of Cream
1 Graham Cracker

Crush Graham Cracker until powder-like. Moisten the rim of a martini glass and coat with Graham Cracker powder (à la the way you would salt a margarita glass rim.)
Add both vodkas to the glass and top with a splash of crème.

A Toast to Jack Lane

The Hollywood Brown Derby was an iconic Hollywood restaurant and later a series of restaurants that went on to inspire the Disney Hollywood Studios restaurant of the same name. Jack Lane was a cartoonist hired by the restaurant who famously would sketch celebrities and the finished portraits lined the walls of the restaurants. Today, replicas of these sketches line the walls of the replica restaurant in WDW as well as a smaller version of the restaurant,

located at the entrance of Walt Disney Studios Park in France. For all who have gandered at the sketches, some of forgotten stars of the past, we say cheers to Jack Lane!

Guy's notes: The story behind the Grapefruit Cake at The Hollywood Brown Derby goes back to the actual restaurant in Hollywood. Gossip columnist Louella Parsons wanted a diet dessert so the chef prepared a dessert that *seemed* healthy. Truthfully, it's full of calories but *tastes* lighter than most cakes.

Space Island Ice Tea

Compare to 'Long Island Lunar Tea' at Sci-Fi Dine-In Theater Restaurant at Disney's Hollywood Studios.

1 oz Bacardi Superior Rum
1 oz Tito's Handmade Vodka
.5 oz Hendrick's gin
.5 oz Cointreau
4 oz sour mix
1 oz Coca-Cola®

Stir in liquors and sour mix into a mixing cup. Pour into an ice tea glass full of ice. Top with Coca-Cola.

A Toast to Richard Hollingshead

Richard Hollingshead was a sales manager for the family auto parts business. His mother was a large woman and was uncomfortable sitting in movie theater seats. Richard had an idea and he began experimenting in his back yard with a movie projector and a bedsheet.
His experiment led to a patent for the first drive-in theater.
Today Disney celebrates this unique invention with an out of this world

restaurant at Disney's Hollywood Studios. This drive in would have never been possible without Richard! Let's raise our glass and say Cheers!

Guy's notes: The Sci-Fi Dine-In Theater Restaurant is not just a unique dining experience, but I believe it's a continuation of Walt's dream for Main Street U.S.A.
When Disneyland opened in 1955, the oldest visitors would have strong memories of a Main Street like that. The middle group would have faint memories and know stories about that style of Main Street and the youngest group would learn about Main Street from Disneyland. The same can be said today about Drive-In Theaters. Many older guests have experienced it and remember it fondly, whereas younger guests have fuzzy memories from childhood or references they heard from television shows. The youngest guests at Sci-Fi have probably never heard of a Drive-In theater. It's great they can experience it at Disney's Hollywood Studios.

Western Sunset

Compare to 'California Sunset' at Baseline Tap House at Disney's Hollywood Studios.

1 oz Absolut Berri Açaí Vodka
1 oz Southern Comfort
2 oz Orange Juice
1 oz sour mix
.5 oz Pomegranate Juice

Mix ingredients and serve in a red wine glass.

A Toast to Edward Wadewitz

In 1907, 30 year old Edward Wadewitz was working for West Side Printing Company. He was told his boss was unable to pay him, so he took his savings and purchased the company. He expanded the company which eventually became known as Western Publishing and became the creator of Little Golden Books.
Under this banner they were the exclusive licensee of Disney titles a relationship that led to them sponsoring the Story Book Shop on Main Street of the, soon to open, Disneyland Park. As the planning of

the park continued Walt Disney needed investors and the company that Edward Wadewitz had founded became part owner of Disneyland Inc. Walt eventually bought out Western Publishing's interest in the park, but today we remember how Edward's vision entertained and enriched the minds of children. To Edward!

Guy's notes: This cocktail is served at the Baseline Tap House which has the fictional Disney backstory of once being home to the Figueroa Printing Company and images adorn the walls to help create that story. Our version has swapped the name of California Sunset for Western Sunset. It's fitting that California's sunset would be in the west, but it also harkens back to Wadewitz's company Western Publishing. The company slowly stopped publishing in the early 1990s and was absorbed into a larger company by the end of that decade.

Animal Kingdom

I didn't have much to say here until I remembered reading an article in National Geographic where it talked about deer eating over ripe apples to get drunk. The next thing I remember I was passed out in the back yard under the apple tree next to a deer named Sammy. He never called me again. Jerk.

This park has changed a whole lot over its relatively short lifespan. The park was opened in 1998 with a design and layout to compliment the theme of animals. It made sense for a company with a mouse as a mascot to try and celebrate the Animal Kingdom. However, over the years the message and theme has gotten a bit watered down. But the booze hasn't! Oh wait, not time for that transition yet. I'll use that later.

The watering down of the Animal Kingdom concept was really noticeable when they added Pandora. What animal are they celebrating? Disney decided the addition of this exciting new land was more important than staying the course with the theme. It really brings home the brilliance with the concept of Disneyland. Having these themed lands like Tomorrowland and Adventureland made it easy to find a way to integrate almost any concept into the vague guidelines of a themed land. Had Walt made the whole park Fantasyland you couldn't just stick a Buzz Lightyear ride there. Or maybe you could. I guess some people have fantasies about Buzz Lightyear. I won't judge them I once fantasized about the pretty dog in *Pound Puppies*. The one with the cute skirt and the flower behind her big floppy ear. So cute.

However, over the years the message and theme has gotten a bit watered down. But the booze hasn't! Yeah, that still works.

Animal Kingdom has lots of fine restaurants with great cocktails as well as some of the most delightful little drink carts you'll find anywhere.

Cryo Rum Slush

Compare to 'Rum Blossom' at Pongu
at Disney's Animal Kingdom Park.

2 oz Bacardi Superior Rum
.5 oz Monin Desert Pear® Syrup
.5 oz Monin Granny Smith Apple Syrup
6 oz Minute Maid lemonade
1/2 cup Passion Fruit Boba Balls

Note: This drink is meant to be
layered, but if you aren't concerned
with presentation you can mix it
together.

Mix 3 oz lemonade with apple syrup and
ice in blender until slushy and put
aside (should look green in color.)
Mix 3 ounces of lemonade with Desert
Pear syrup and ice in blender until
slushy (should be purple) and pour
half in large fountain glass. Layer
the green on top and then layer the
remaining purple slush.
Float the rum and Boba Balls on top.

A Toast to Glenn Langan

The handsome actor, Glenn Langan, appeared in dozens of Hollywood roles in his 39 year career. He made small appearances on *Gilligan's Island*, *The Danny Thomas Show* and *Hondo*. But it was his 1957 role as *The Amazing Colossal Man* that endeared him to science fiction film fans. The iconic American International Pictures film became a drive-in hit, so it's fitting that the trailer for this film plays many times a day at Sci-Fi Dine-In Theater at Disney's Hollywood Studios. So, let's raise this colossal cocktail and scream like a giant man injected with an oversized hypodermic needle! To Glenn!

Guy's notes: I'm not gonna lie, your drink probably isn't going to look as nice as the drink at Animal Kingdom. However, if you mix it right it will taste just as good. So mix one up, turn on *Avatar*, dim the lights and drink it in the dark!

Hightower's Thunder

Compare to 'Hightower Rocks' at Nomad Lounge at Disney's Animal Kingdom

2 oz Blanco Tequila
2 oz Sweet-and-Sour
1 oz Watermelon juice
1 oz Lime Juice

Mix tequila, lime juice and sweet and sour in a cocktail shaker with cracked ice.
Add watermelon juice to rocks glass and pour cocktail shaker on top.
Garnish with small watermelon wedge.

A Toast to Bubba Smith

Bubba Smith was a defensive end for Baltimore, Oakland and Houston before retiring and becoming an actor. His best known role was as Hightower in the Police Academy series, so it's fitting that this cocktail be raised to him. Bubba passed away in 2011 and his career didn't have much connection to Disney, but in 1984 he starred in the ABC TV series Blue Thunder about the coolest helicopter since Airwolf

(also 1984.)
A prop Blue Thunder helicopter was in the boneyard on the Disney-MGM Studios backlot tour. Let's raise a glass to Bubba Smith!

Guy's notes: This is a good drink to put together when you are at a summer picnic. Just grab an oz of watermelon juice from the bottom of a bowl of watermelon slices. Otherwise, you can buy bottled watermelon juice at your grocery store, but make sure it's not full of added sugars. Disney makes this cocktail with Casa Dragones Blanco Tequila, but you can use any blanco or silver tequila (Don Julio is easy to find.)
Blanco tequila is clear because it is aged less than other types of tequila which get a darker tint from the wood barrel it's aged in.

Jenn's Mom's Embarrassment

Compare to 'Jenn's Tattoo' at Tiffins Restaurant at Disney's Animal Kingdom Theme Park.

2 oz Ketel One Vodka
4 oz Fruit Punch flavored Gatorade
1 oz Hibiscus syrup
1 oz Lime Juice
1 Hibiscus flower in syrup

Add the hibiscus syrup, Gatorade and vodka in a shaker and shake with ice. Pour into Collins glass over ice and stir in lime juice. Garnish with lime wedge with Hibiscus flower floating on top.

A Toast to Mary Blair

Mary Blair was an artist and designer well known by Disney fans. Her iconic designs for "It's a Small World" and the enormous mosaic at the Contemporary Resort are favorites among Disney fans. However, we are toasting her for the design of Jenny in the Disney flick *Melody Time*.

In the film Jenny and her boyfriend Joe go ice skating with, the less skilled, Jenny falling behind and getting annoyed at her cheeky beau.

Mary designed Jenny (along with Fred Moore) and Mary could have also designed a tattoo that even Jenn's mom would be proud of.

Guy's notes: The version at Tiffins uses a watermelon juice, but it really gave me a Gatorade vibe so I tried it and found it to be an excellent (and more widely available) substitute.

The Hibiscus syrup is available online. There a brand named "Wild Hibiscus" that cooks them in the jar and vacuum seals them for a long shelf life. The flowers come in the syrup.

Disney's version is garnished with a hibiscus flower floating on a small lime wheel.

You can be classy like that. Or just float the Gatorade cap in your drink like a boss.

Moharaza's Limearita

Compare to 'Maharaja Lime Margarita'
at
Warung Outpost at Disney's Animal
Kingdom Theme Park.

1 oz Sauza Silver Tequila
1 oz Triple Sec
1 tbsp agave syrup
2 oz fresh lime juice

Combine agave syrup and lime juice
and shake well. Mix in Triple Sec and
pour into iced margarita glass with
salted rim. Float tequila on top.
Garnish with lime wedge.

A Toast to Phil Harris Phil
Harris was a comedian and jazz
singer known for his voice work in
several Disney films, most notably
as Baloo the bear in *The Jungle
Book*.
Phil was born to a pair of circus
performers and worked as a drummer in
the circus as a youth. He became a
bandleader in the 1920s and in 1942
he and his band enlisted in the U.S.
Navy and served in World War II.

His is a life well regarded and well-remembered. To Phil Harris!

Guy's notes: Maharajah is a title meaning "great king" and Moharaza is an alternate spelling that I really like.
This is a pretty standard Margarita, but the agave nectar is a great substitute for simple syrup. It's sweeter and a bit more complex of a flavoring.
This drink is served at the Warung Outpost. It's a nice little stand with an interesting name. Warung is a word used in Indonesia to describe a small convenience shop that a family opens in front of their home.
These are often made from bamboo or thatch. The Disney location is mostly wood with some decorative lattice and some small tables on the side.
It's a real great place to enjoy a drink.

Disney Springs

Disney Springs may not sound correct to you. You may be thinking "Disney Springs? How does Disney have the season of spring multiple times?" Well, you're not thinking of it correctly. Maybe you're thinking "The only Springs I know about at Disney were the springs in the mattress I slept on. They kept biting me." Well, I'm gonna have to ask you to stop thinking about stupid things like that because this is about Disney Springs. Also, check yourself for bed bug bites.

The real reason Disney Springs sounds wrong is that the area has had so many different names over the years. People still call it Downtown Disney or Disney Village or Disney Marketplace. Whatever you call it, don't call it late for dinner! No, that's silly. They serve dinner really late here. I'm starting to think I may have malaria. Do bed bugs cause malaria?

Disney Springs is divided into a bunch of different sections including Town Center and West Side. They have renamed the sections from time to time, too so you may think of an area as Pleasure Island or some other name from the past. We should all stop thinking and start drinking.

The backstory of Disney Springs is that it was settled by a cattle rancher named Martin Sinclair in 1850. Martin was married to a woman named Clara. This backstory is detailed in the restaurant D-Luxe Burger (which is supposed to be the ranch house.)

I like that they are named Marty and Clara. It's like if *Back to the Future part III* had taken a weird turn. You know, Buford "Mad Dog" Tannen guns down Doc and Marty has to comfort Clara. One thing leads to another and then they have a little May-December romance and then ZZ Top played at the wedding.

Well, on that note, enjoy the Disney Springs cocktails!

Bourbon Shakin' With Bacon

Compare to 'Smoked Bourbon Gelato Shake' at D-Luxe Burger at Disney Springs.

3 scoops Talenti Vanilla Bean Gelato
2 oz Knob Creek Bourbon
1 tsp Liquid Smoke
.5 cup milk
.25 cup Hershey's Special Dark Chocolate Syrup
Strip of cooked bacon

Blend gelato and milk until smooth. Add dark chocolate sauce and liquid smoke and blend for another 10 seconds.
Place cooked bacon straight up in tall milkshake glass and pour in, leaving just the top 2 inches of bacon above the milkshake. Float the bourbon on top.

A Toast to Veryl Waldron In November of 1983 Veryl and her husband Bill saw a man carrying a rifle on the second floor of The Sands Motel, across the street from Disneyland. She notified the manager and led to the arrest of the sniper, but not before he fired 13 rounds towards nearby motels and Disneyland. Thankfully for Veryl's call for help, Anaheim P.D. was on the scene fast to subdue the sniper and no one was killed. Cheers to the memory of Veryl Waldron!

Guy's notes: D-Luxe doesn't float the Bourbon, but I like to float it. That way the drink gets stronger as you get close to the end. Or if you can't finish it, you can gulp down that great Knob Creek and toss aside the milkshake. This calls for gelato instead of ice cream. Gelato is actually the Italian word for 'ice cream,' but the gelato sold in the USA is usually denser than ice cream which packs a tight milkshake. Liquid smoke is an acquired taste, but I like it. Gives a hickory flavor to everything. I love to add a few drops to chili or hamburgers, but I never thought I'd get to put it in a cocktail or a milkshake.

Brontosaurus' Banana

Compare to 'Caveman Punch' at
T-REX ™ at Disney Springs.

1 oz Captain Morgan's Spiced Rum
1 oz 99 Bananas
1 oz DeKuyper Peachtree Schnapps
4 oz Tropicana Twister Fruit Punch
Juice

Combine rum, 99 Bananas, Peachtree
Schnapps and fruit punch in a
cocktail shaker with ice and shake
vigorously. Pour into frosted beer
mug and garnish with a quarter of a
peeled banana with an umbrella
pierced through the top.

A Toast to Winsor McCay

No discussion of the history of
animation can be had without starting
with Winsor McCay.
McCay started illustrating newspapers
and magazines in the late 1800s and
pioneered the world of animation in
the 1910s.
His character Gertie the Dinosaur was
a huge hit and the first animated
star.

Walt Disney featured Gertie and McCay in an episode of the Disneyland TV series and Disney Hollywood Studios has a giant googie-style building shaped like Gertie, home of 'Dinosaur Gertie's Ice Cream of Extinction.' Let's toast Winsor McCay!

Guy's notes: Tropicana Twister is a pretty easy to find fruit juice and it makes for a nice base to the drink. 99 Bananas is pretty awful and overpowers everything it touches, but the sugar in Tropicana Twister does a good job of smoothing things out. It's a silly drink, but it pairs well with a viewing of any monster movie on a late summer night.

Bulleit and Blood

Compare to 'Blood Orange Bourbon' at Raglan Road Irish Pub and Restaurant at Disney Springs.

1 oz Bulleit Bourbon
1 oz Nolet's Gin
1 oz San Pellegrino Blood Orange

Stir in ingredients and serve over ice in rocks glass.

A Toast to Michael Graves

Michael Graves was a world-famous architect. He designed several buildings for Disney including the studio headquarters in Burbank and the iconic Swan and Dolphin hotels on Disney's Boardwalk. He also designed numerous kitchen products for Target and J.C. Penney.
In 2003 Graves became partially paralyzed due to a spinal cord infection. He continued working and designed wheelchairs and hospital furnishings. To a man who truly made the world more beautiful, we raise a glass to Michael Graves!

Guy's notes: Raglan Road has a unique gimmick. They built the bar in Ireland and then disassembled it and shipped it to America for it to be reassembled in Disney Springs.
If you drank there, you truly drank at a real Irish pub.
One of the details I like of Raglan Road is that they recordings of Irish comedians playing in the bathrooms. It sure helps pass the time.
If you want to try this at home read this joke aloud from the great Irish comedian Hal Roach as you… you know… go.

"Daddy, is it true we come from dust and to dust we shall return?" His father said, "'Tis true. Why do you ask?" And the kid said, "Well, you better look under my bed. There's somebody there either comin' or goin'." Hal Roach (1988)

Dapper

Compare to 'Flawless' at STK Orlando at Disney Springs.

2 oz Grey Goose vodka
3 oz lemon juice
2 oz raspberry juice
1 oz prosecco

Mix ingredients (except prosecco) in a shaker with ice. Strain and serve in a red wine glass. Stir in prosecco.

A Toast to Johnny Carson

Johnny Carson was the host of The Tonight Show for almost 30 years. His tenure on the show included numerous guests promoting Disney films and lots of comedy segments skewering The Disney Company.
However, it was a 1974 musician strike that gave Johnny an indelible tie to Disneyland. As the regular band of The Tonight Show was abiding the strike, Johnny brought on the Disney barbershop quartet, The Dapper Dans, to be a replacement band. Being an acapella group The Dapper Dans didn't have to cross the picket line to perform. As a result, millions of late

night viewers were serenaded by the beautiful sounds that are usually only found on Main Street U.S.A. For this moment in time we remember the great Johnny Carson!

Guy's notes: Carson often had lots of Disney segments. One segment in 1990 featured Rejected Disney Characters including Dumpo the Flying Elephant, Stinkerbell, model Jessica Hahn as Bimbi and a Fox and the Hound parody featuring Redd Foxx and the "Tax Hounds." It's funnier if you're old.

I always recommend squeezing your own fruit juices. Raspberries are a little tougher to juice if you don't like the seeds. Personally I don't mind them, but if you get annoyed by them get a very fine strainer or a coffee filter and strain the juice before you serve it.

Easy Green

Compare to 'Green Intensity' at
STK Orlando at Disney Springs.

2 oz Ketel One Citroen Vodka
.5 oz St~Germain Elderflower Liqueur
1/3 of a cucumber
Mint leaves

Completely peel cucumber and muddle
with mint leaves. Strain and discard
pulp.
Pour into martini glass and add St-
Germain and Ketel One. Garnish with
cucumber slice.

A Toast to Betty Henson

Betty Henson was the mother of Muppets
creator Jim Henson. Legend has it that
Betty's old coat was used by Jim to
create the very first Kermit the Frog.
In reality Kermit wasn't officially a
frog at first. Originally Kermit
lacked his trademarked pointed collar
and was considered to be a lizard-eque
creature.
For many year's Kermit's green face
adorned a large (faux) hot air balloon
outside Muppet Vision 3D, Kermit has

starred in numerous films and TV shows and his song "The Rainbow Connection" reached number 25 on the Billboard Hot 100. Perhaps none of the accolades would exist if Betty Henson hadn't decided to buy and later discard a green spring coat. Let's raise this green cocktail to Betty and her coat!

Guy's notes: The presentation of this one at STK is really unique. They take a (lengthwise) very thin slice of the cucumber about 8 inches in length. The slice has dark green of the peel on both sides and the light green of the inner layer.
They then ribbon this on a toothpick so it looks almost like a green piece of bacon.
It's beautiful, but don't waste your time with making one yourself. What you should do instead is attach two black olives to two toothpicks and stick them through a cucumber slice to make a garnish that evokes Kermit the Frog.

Lunar Saunter

Compare to 'The Moonwalk'
Stargazers at Disney Springs.

1 oz SKYY Infusions Blood Orange Vodka
1 oz SKYY Infusions Pineapple Vodka
2 oz Orange Juice
1 oz Pineapple Juice
1 oz Sprite

Mix your ingredients (except Sprite) in a shaker full of ice and shake gently. Pour into cocktail glass, add more ice and top with Sprite. Garnish with orange wheel.

A Toast to Neil Armstrong

In June of 1969 Neil Armstrong became the first human being to walk on the moon. That moment was captured and broadcast live. Today the footage plays in multiple Disney attractions including The American Adventure and Spaceship Earth.
Walt Disney died three years before Armstrong's walk, but Walt had spent many of the last years of his life fascinated with space travel. Walt created episodes of his "Disneyland" TV series titled "Man in Space" and

"Man and the Moon" that took a
serious look at space travel. At the
Disneyland theme park he created
Flight to the Moon, an attraction
that gave guests the thrill of space
travel.

It seemed fitting that when Space
Mountain had a grand re-opening in
2005, Neil Armstrong was there for
the dedication.

It is for these "out of this world"
reasons that we drink a toast to the
original Moonwalker and Lunar
Saunterer, Neil Armstrong!

Guy's notes: Neil Armstrong's "One
Small Step…" quote is engraved on a
tile outside Mission Space in EPCOT.
The Disney version of this cocktail
shares a name with The Moonwalk
cocktail invented by Joe Gilmore. Joe
was the longest serving bartender at
The Savoy Hotel and invented the
drink to be the first drink Neil
Armstrong and Buzz Aldrin would have
once they returned to earth. The
Disney version has different
ingredients but a similar taste.

Pinocchios over Manhattan

Compare to '...Not Your Daddy's Manhattan' at STK Orlando at Disney Springs.

2 oz Woodford Reserve Bourbon
1 oz Carpano Antica Sweet Vermouth
2 dashes Peychaud's Bitters
1 Maraschino cherry
1 Orange twist

Combine in a shaker with ice. Put the cherry at the bottom of a chilled goblet glass and strain cocktail over top. Garnish with orange twist.

A Toast to Samuel L. Rothafel

Samuel "Roxy" Rothafel was a silent movie producer and promotor of lavish movie palaces of the 1920s. He opened the Roxy Theater in Times Square as well as the Radio City Music Hall and the Center Theater.
The Center Theatre lasted just over 20 years before it's demolition in 1954, making it the only original Rockefeller Center complex to see a wrecking ball. It was at the Center Theatre where an unusual Disney event happened. For the opening of

Pinocchio, Disney hired a team of dwarfs to wear Pinocchio masks and wave from the top of the marquee. Legend has it that after a few hours the performers got drunk, stripped naked and burped loudly as they played craps. Police were called to carry the nude dwarfs down in pillowcases.
It's a great story and without Roxy's theater we wouldn't have this story!
To Roxy!

Guy's notes: The story of the drunken dwarves was misreported for years as being at the premiere of *Snow White and the Seven Dwarfs* (for obvious reasons.)
In recent years a photo of the dwarves has surfaced but it shows happy and well behaved dwarves waving to the crowd. It's hard to imagine that, even if they were pants-less or shooting dice, anyone would be able to tell based on the height of the marquee railing.
But, it's a fun story.

Prosecco You Face

Compare to 'Holly Hill' at Enzo's
Hideaway at Disney Springs.

1 oz Ketel One Vodka
1 oz St~Germain liqueur
4 oz Seltzer water
1 oz Prosecco

Pour cold seltzer and prosecco into a
saucer-style margarita glass. Stir in
vodka and liqueur and garnish with a
lemon peel.

A Toast to Herman 'Kay' Kamen

In the 1930s The Waterbury Clock
Company was approached by Kay Kamen, a
licensing agent from the Disney
Company. Kay wanted to make Mickey
Mouse watches. Even Walt Disney
thought this idea was a dud, but it
went on to become a rousing success
and Mickey Mouse watches became almost
as iconic as Mickey Mouse himself.
To Herman Kay Kamen. Without him, we'd
never know what time it is!

Guy's notes: The story of the Mickey Mouse watch makes me think of an observation I had years ago.

I often hear the term "Mickey Mouse _____" when the item in question is cheap or poorly made.

I imagine the origin of this term is these low cost, popular watches. What makes the phrase so antiquated now is that Mickey Mouse (and the Disney Company) are rarely connected to something cheap.

Disney vacation destinations are known for their high cost and many consumers place a high confidence in the Disney Company when they are purchasing all kinds of products.

T.A.E

Compare to 'The Edison' at The Edison at Disney Springs.

1 oz Woodford Reserve Bourbon
1 oz Belle de Brillet Pear Brandy
1 oz Lemon Juice
1 oz Belvoir Honey Lemon Ginger Cordial

Add ice and mix and shake until frothy. Strain into a sherry glass.

A Toast to Thomas Edison

Thomas Alva Edison was an American inventor and businessman. We all have heard of his inventions that included the electric light bulb, the phonograph and the motion picture camera.

In 1998 his Edison Lamp Company merged with Drexel, Morgan & Co. to create General Electric. It is truly fitting that Carousel of Progress, an attraction that got its start as a General Electric sponsored show, features the line "Mr. Edison sure added life to our home."

So let's all snap on some electric lights and raise a glass to Thomas

Alva Edison who has added life to all our homes!

Guy's notes: This is a nice cocktail. Complex flavors but really easy to make. You can sub whatever whiskey you have for the bourbon, but you'll need to get Pear Brandy and I find that Belle de Brillet is good and about as easy to find as any other.

The Edison is a fun place to go to at Disney Springs. It's enormous. The atmosphere at night is electric (as Edison would want it) but I prefer the laid back atmosphere you can find there at lunch time.

In additional to the mentions in Carousel of Progress you can find Susan B. Anthony shouting about him in American Adventure and see information about him and his inventions in the lobby of the attraction.

There was an unbuilt section of Disneyland that Walt imagined called Edison Square and an early proposal for Horizons was that it would be all about Edison and his inventions.

THE REST OF WALT DISNEY WORLD

Walt Disney World is huge. By any reasonable standard it is enormous.

There are countless bars where you can get a cocktail. That's not really true, I guess you could count them if you wanted. If you had a cocktail at each one you'd be pretty drunk before you got to each of the bars and drunk people can't count as good as sober people.

You might want to try going to the bars and only order a soda or something like that. If you want the bartender to think you're a tough guy ordering a soda, order it like this: "Hey barkeep, fetch me a whiskey… no wait, make it a soda pop. But serve it in a dirty glass."

The bars in Walt Disney World are in some pretty unique places. Disney's Boardwalk is a wonderful place. It's located just outside of EPCOT Center and it has the feel of an old timey seaside boardwalk area. Without the sea part.

Outside the Magic Kingdom you have the Seven Seas Lagoon which is bordered by Disney's Contemporary Resort, Disney's Grand Floridian Resort & Spa and Disney's Polynesian Resort. These hotels are all on a monorail loop. For a fun time outside the park you can bar hop from place to place enjoying drinks at Outer Rim, Trader Sam's Grog Grotto and that Beauty and the Beast bar that replaced Mizner's Lounge.

While you are there, raise your glass to Addison Mizner, the architect who's Spanish Colonial Revival style beautified Palm Beach and Boca Raton.

Then you can ponder why Boca Raton has that name at all when it's Spanish for "rat's mouth." Then raise a glass to rats like you and I.

Walt Disney World has some other great places to get drinks to pour into your Boca Raton. You can experience the serene Fort Wilderness area or the excitement of the water parks.

It's a cornucopia of cocktails. And corn, too. You can buy corn niblets all over WDW.

I have compiled some of my favorite recipes in this chapter (for cocktails, not niblets.)

Black Magic Gimlet

Compare to 'Magical Star Cocktail' at Whispering Canyon Cafe at Disney's Wilderness Lodge.

1.5 oz X-Rated Fusion Liqueur
.5 oz Parrot Bay Coconut Rum
4 oz Pineapple Juice

Mix all ingredients in a shaker with ice. Pour into a cosmo glass.

A Toast to Ed Moriarty

One of the first cast members hired for Walt Disney World in Orlando, Ed Moriarty certainly made an impact on the Florida resort. Moriarty wanted to bring a destination shopping area to WDW and worked to create the Lake Buena Vista Shopping Village which is today known as Disney Springs. Moriarty saw the need for some areas of Walt Disney World to be for adults and brought more sophisticated shopping and dining to this part of Walt Disney World, including a high end men's store which paid tribute to Ed with its name, Sir Edward's Haberdashery.

It is with great respect that we hold our glasses high to Sir Edward!

Guy's notes: For obvious reasons, Disney lists "X-Rated Fusion Liqueur" as "X-Fusion Organic Mango and Passion Fruit Liqueur" on their menus and website.

Disney serves this with a glow cube which always makes a drink more fun.

On the subject of Ed Moriarty, Ed retired from Disney at age 45. He left to take it easy and enjoy his family. Years later he returned to work as president of the Ron Jon Surf Shop company. A few months after Ed's death in 2018 Disney announced that Ron Jon Surf Shop would be opening a store in Disney Springs. It's nice to see a union of the two brands Ed worked so passionately for.

Buena Vista Home Video

Compare to 'Buena Vista' at Capa at Four Seasons Resort Orlando at Walt Disney World Resort.

2 oz Tanteo - Jalapeno Infused Tequila
2 oz Torres Magdala Orange Liqueur
Sprinkle of Espelette pepper powder
Salt Air (salt foam, see directions below)

Mix the Tanteo and Magdala in a cocktail shaker with ice. Strain and pour into wide mouthed champagne saucer. Cover with Salt Air and sprinkle Espellette pepper powder on top (or substitute with chili powder.)

Salt Air (prepared in separate shaker)
3 oz water
2 oz lime juice
3 tsp of maltodextrin
2 tsp salt
Mix ingredients in cocktail shaker and shake vigorously. Spoon out foam on top of cocktail.

A Toast to Kenjiro Takayanagi

The Disney version of this cocktail is named after the street in Burbank, California where the Disney studio is located, but our version is named after the once ubiquitous VHS label owned by the Disney Company, Buena Vista Home Video. Therefore, we toast to Kenjiro Takayanagi.

Kenjiro was called "the father of Japanese television" and had developed the first all-electronic television set in 1926. Later, as Vice President of JVC, he pushed for affordable video tape recorders and they developed a two head video cassette recorder in 1959. Kenjiro passed away in 1990, but his legacy lives on in the VHS copies of *Return of Jafar* and *Sing-Along Songs: Campout at Walt Disney World* filling the shelves at thrift stores across America! Raise a glass, and an un-rewound tape to Kenjiro Takayanagi!

Guy's notes: This is intended to be a very high end cocktail and Capa uses some high end ingredients. They use Casamigos - Reposado Tequila, but Tanteo provides the same impact in the drink with less impact to the wallet.

Comfort in a Hurricane

Compare to 'Southern Hurricane' at Scat Cat's Club at Disney's Port Orleans Resort - French Quarter.

1 oz Myers's Original Dark Rum
1 oz Don Q Cristal Rum
.5 oz Southern Comfort
3 oz Orange juice
2 oz Welch's Passion Fruit Cocktail

Shake all ingredients (except Southern Comfort) in a cocktail shaker with ice and strain into a hurricane glass filled with ice. Float Southern Comfort on top. Garnish with orange slice.

A Toast to Mr. Feuchtwanger

The history of the hot dog is as murky as a pot of water after a batch of hot dogs are boiled. Sausages similar to our hot dogs have had a place in history going back hundreds of years. Some historians credit a German immigrant named Feuchtwanger with first selling hot dogs on rolls in the Midwest in the late 1800s. Prior to that, patrons were given gloves so the hot dogs would burn their hands. The story says that many patrons didn't return the gloves and so Mr. Feuchtwanger and his wife decided to start serving the hot dogs on buns.

Today, on Main Street U.S.A., a staple food of Disney fans is the hot dogs at Casey's Corner. Hot dogs have long been considered a part of Americana so it's no surprise that they are featured here. Let's raise a glass (or a dog) to Mr. Feuchtwanger!

Guy's notes: Casey's Corner is located in Magic Kingdom and in Disneyland Paris. I think it's great that we have brought this fine eatery to France. The restaurant is based on "Casey at the Bat" which is a poem first published in 1888. Disney animated a version of the story in the package film *Make Mine Music* (1946.)

Destino Gin Tonic

Compare to 'Gran Gin Tonic' at Barcelona Lounge at Disney's Coronado Springs Resort.

2 oz Gabriel Boudier Safron Infused Gin
3 lime wedges
1 orange peel
2 oz tonic

Add gin to highball glass filled with ice cubes and orange peel. Squeeze 3 lime wedges and into glass and add them to glass. Mix in tonic and stir gently.

A Toast to Salvador Dalí

Famed artist Salvador Dalí was known for is surreal artwork. It was a distinctive look that people recognized. Walt Disney was an artist whose work also had a distinctive look that was recognized immediately.
In 1945 the two worked together on a collaboration. After eight months of Disney artist John Hench working closely with Dali the project was put

on hold and eventually scrapped. However, in 1999 the project was revisited. The end result was a seven minute short film that played in art museums and film festivals. That film, *Destino*, inspired the look and name of the Gran Destino Tower at Disney's Coronado Springs Resort. So we drop our paintbrushes and raise our glass and say "salud!" to Salvador Dalí!

Guy's notes: The Gran Gin and Tonic is a marvelous drink. It is the signature drink at the Gran Destino Tower at Disney's Coronado Springs Resort. The Disney version uses the more traditional Tanqueray London Dry Gin but they also use a house made saffron-orange tonic. You can make your own if you purchase saffron threads, but I found the Gabriel Boudier Safron Infused Gin to work to replicate what that delicious Gran Gin Tonic tasted like.

Dircksian Phantasmagoria

Compare to 'Pepper's Ghost' at
Abracadabar at Disney's BoardWalk.

2 oz Ciroc Pineapple Vodka
1 oz Monin Habanero Lime Syrup
1 oz Lime juice
1 dash Bittermens Hellfire Habanero
Shrub
Crushed black pepper
Pineapple cube

Combine vodka, syrup and lime in a
shaker filled with ice. Shake and
strain into a saucer margarita
glass. Add a dash of Bittermens
Hellfire Habanero Shrub and crushed
black pepper. Coat pineapple cube
with pepper and add to drink (on
large toothpick) as a garnish.

A Toast to Henry Dircks

The Pepper's Ghost effect is a
projection technique that is used
heavily in the Haunted Mansion.
Pepper's Ghost is named for John Henry
Pepper who popularized a working
version of the effect. Pepper didn't
want the technique named for him

because he wanted credit to be given to its inventor, Henry Dircks. Dircks had named it Dircksian Phantasmagoria. Pepper and Dircks shared credit on the patent but Dircks signed over all financial rights to idea to Pepper. It is because of these two friends that we have this magical effect at Disney parks! Today let's toast to Henry Dircks!

Guy's notes: This drink is really amazing. As always, use real lime juice. Disney's version doesn't use the Bittermens Hellfire Habanero Shrub (as far as I know) but it gives it a great kick.

Many Disney fans are aware of the term "Pepper's Ghost" but outside of Disney circles it's less well known. Pepper's Ghost was used to make Tupac appear onstage, but it was widely reported as a high tech hologram.

Pepper's Ghost is also used in modern Teleprompters.

Hero's Welcome

Compare to 'Black Cherry Lemonade' at Polar Pub at Disney's Blizzard Beach Water Park.

2 oz Grey Goose Cherry Noir Vodka
3 oz Odwalla Lemonade
1 oz Lime Juice
1 oz Grenadine
.5 oz Sprite

Add all ingredients in a blender (except Sprite) with a cup of ice. Blend until slushy and pour into glass. Top with Sprite and garnish with a lime wedge.

A Toast to Hero of Alexandria

The term Audio-Animatronics was coined and is trademarked by The Walt Disney Company. The initial versions were animated pneumatic actuators that would move the various parts of the robotic characters via hydraulics. This is what causes the mechanical popping noises you can hear when you listen closely on It's a Small World or Country Bear Jamboree.
The history of pneumatic actuators can

be traced back to 71 AD to an Egyptian mathematician named Hero.
Hero created the first steam engine, the force pump and the first vending machine (it dispensed Holy Water for a coin.)

Perhaps Hero's most Walt Disney-esque invention was a mechanical theatrical play powered by system of ropes and simple machines operated by a rotating cylindrical cogwheel.
It's because of inventors like Hero that we have had dolls from all around the world sing a song of peace. To Hero!

Guy's notes: Disney's version is called Black Cherry Lemonade, but that's not really true. It's really lemonade and grenadine.
The name grenadine comes from the French word for pomegranate. Original recipes included pomegranate, sugar and water. Most off the shelf grenadine you'll buy today has high fructose corn syrup and other stuff you'd usually find in sugary sodas.

Ice Gator Margarita

Compare to 'Blue Blizzard Margarita' at Polar Pub at Disney's Blizzard Beach Water Park.

1 cup Herradura Reposado Tequila
.5 cup Blue Curaçao
.5 cup Sweet-and-Sour
6 cups ice

Makes 4. Add tequila, Blue Curaçao, sweet and sour and ice into a blender and blend until smooth. Pour and serve immediately.

A Toast to Budge Brown

Robert "Budge" Brown owned a small water park in California in 1975. At that time water slides were made of concrete and riders would slide down on a mat. Budge was disappointed with the slow pace of waterslides and came up with the novel innovation of using an all fiberglass slide which allowed waterslides to reach speeds never before possible and eliminating the necessity of a mat. Budge Brown's ideas have substantially changed water attractions at Disney parks and everywhere else around the world. Let us raise a glass to Budge Brown!

Guy's notes: Ice Gator is the blue alligator that serves as the mascot for Blizzard Beach Water Park. Disney loves to create elaborate backstories for their parks, rides, hotels etc., and these backstories are rarely known by the average guest. The legend behind Blizzard Beach was that a ski resort had been built after a freak snowstorm in Orlando but was on the brink of closure when the snow melted. However, Ice Gator was spotted sliding down a flume screaming "Yahoo!" inspiring the change from ski resort to water park. You can't really blend this right unless you are making a batch for four so find some friends to drink it with you. If you can't find any friends, don't be sad. That's four for you and none for those losers.
You can salt the rim of your glasses if you like or if your friends like salt on the rim. Or if you can't find any friends get liquored up and then throw salt in those loser's eyes like Mr. Fuji at Wrestlemania IX.

mooberry

Compare to 'zooberry' at
Todd English's bluezoo at Walt
Disney World Swan and Dolphin
Resort.

2 oz SKYY Infusions Blueberry Vodka
2 oz Fresh Lemon Juice
2 oz Fee Brothers Rock Candy Simple
Bar Syrup

Fill cosmo glass halfway with crushed
ice, mix ingredients in shaker and
add to glass. Garnish with toothpick
holding Gummy Milky Cow Candy and a
blueberry.

A Toast to Dorothy Jean Brockberg

Dororthy Brockberg was a stay at home
mother who lived on a farm near
Trosky, Minnesota with her husband
Melvin.
On the family farm was a cow born with
spots that bore a striking resemblance
to the silhouette of Mickey Mouse. The
Disney Company purchased the cow, then
named Minnie Moo, and she lived out
her life at Mickey's Starland and Tri-
Circle D Ranch at Fort Wilderness.

Thanks to Dorothy and her family this cow brought a little extra magic to Walt Disney World. To Dorothy!

Guy's notes: This is the signature drink at bluezoo and is served with an orange twist. I've rethemed this to Minnie Moo, so this we garnish with a small gummy cow. You can certainly try the cocktail without the cow, but then you might incur the wrath of a cow ghost and I find that terrifying.
Rock Candy Simple Syrup is a bit sweeter and thicker than your average simple syrup. Fee Brothers makes a good one with no grit and a great taste.

National Forest Cocktail

Compare to 'Mountain Trail Cocktail' at Whispering Canyon Cafe at Disney's Wilderness Lodge.

1 oz Moonshine Whiskey
1 oz Chambord
.5 oz Leroux Blackberry Brandy
3 oz Odwalla lemonade

Mix ingredients in a shaker and pour into a highball glass full of ice. Top with a wild blackberry.

A Toast to Franklin A. Boole

The Boole Tree is a giant sequoia tree that is the largest tree within the U.S. Forest Service.
Franklin was a supervisor of a logging operation that should have cut down the tree. However, Boole was impressed by its size and spared the tree.
Later, a doctor heard the story and named the tree after Boole.
Disney parks have long shown a love for National Parks with resorts like Fort Wilderness and Wilderness Lodge and it is great to remember people that have chosen to appreciate nature. So we raise our cups and shout "Here!

Here!" for Franklin Boole and The Boole Tree!

Guy's notes: This is a great drink and will make you want a refill or two.

Disney's connection to nature extends back to Walt himself. In 1955 he was awarded the Audubon Medal, the highest awards from the National Audubon Society.

Disney received this award because of a long running film series Disney produced called True-Life Adventures. These fun and folksy documentaries showed viewers a rare look at nature. Perhaps the most unique of these programs was *Perri*, a 1957 film that was labeled a True Life Fantasy.

Perri follows a sweet narrative story about a young squirrel that lives her life in the forest.

The film was based on a story by Felix Salten, the author who also created *Bambi*.

The Old GT

Compare to 'Elderflower G&T' at Rix Sports Bar & Grill at Disney's Coronado Springs Resort

3 oz Uncle Val's Botanical Gin
4 oz Jack Rudy's Elderflower Tonic
3 lime wedges Splash of
club soda

Add gin to highball glass filled with ice cubes. Squeeze 3 lime wedges into glass and add them to glass. Mix in tonic and stir gently.

A Toast to Michael Roarty

Michael Roarty was a marketing executive for the Anheuser-Busch brewing company. In the early 1950s, Roarty worked hyping the beer at taverns in Detroit. Local bar owners called him "Mr. Budweiser."
During his long career he assisted in the creation of Spuds MacKenzie and created the slogan "This Bud's for you."
In 1980 he convinced the other big wigs at Bud to give a million dollars to the struggling start up

ESPN. Years later ESPN became a part of the Disney Empire and has a large presence at WDW with the ESPN Wide World of Sports.

Before we sip this cocktail, let's raise the glass to Michael Roarty!

Guy's notes: You can sub in Hendrick's Gin if you can't find Uncle Val's. This tonic is made with quinine and has a very floral aroma. Fever-Tree and Q also offer an Elderflower tonic, but grab Jack Rudy's if possible.
The size of the splash of club soda is up to you, I but I found a big splash evens this out well.
If you're curious about the namesake of Jack Rudy's Elderflower Tonic, it's not Jack RUBY, the man who killed Lee Harvey Oswald. The Jack Rudy company is a family run company based in South Carolina and Kentucky. The founders named the company after their great-grandfather. This Jack Ruby was also apparently a fascinating man. The company website notes that he invented a device for pharmacists to count pills and "was known to overindulge in drink, smoke, and his wife's gourmet cooking."

The Pimlico Cosmo

Compare to 'The Preakness Cosmo' at The Turf Club Lounge at Disney's Saratoga Springs Resort & Spa.

1 oz Smirnoff Citrus Vodka
1 oz Triple Sec
4 oz Cranberry Juice

Combine vodka, Triple Sec and cranberry juice in a cocktail shaker with ice and shake vigorously. Strain into a martini glass and garnish with orange peel.

A Toast to Eric Hatch

Eric Hatch was an American novelist born in 1901. He started a career on Wall Street but it was interrupted by World War II. At the end of combat he returned to work but started writing. His notable works include the screenplay for *Topper* and the novel *My Many Godfrey*.

He also wrote the book *The Year of the Horse* His which was turned into a Disney film under the name *The Horse in the Gray Flannel Suit*.

The story is about a man named Fred

who deals with his problems at work and his adorable daughter who wants a horse.

Hold up your cocktail, shout "...and they're off!" as you put this Cosmo down the hatch in honor of Eric Hatch!

Guy's notes: Pimlico Race Course in Baltimore, Maryland is the home of the Preakness Stakes, a famous horse race that has run since 1873. The race did not run from 1891 to 1893 (the year Roy O. Disney was born.) The Cosmopolitan is said to have been created by a bartender named Neal Murray in 1975 at a steak house in Minneapolis. However, the recipe is very similar to a cocktail – also named Cosmopolitan – in a 1934 book *Pioneers of Mixing at Elite Bars 1903- 1933*.
The winner of the Preakness that year was a horse named High Quest and surely anyone drinking these is on a High Quest indeed!

Ruby Red Rita

Compare to 'Grapefruit Margarita' at Polar Pub at Disney's Blizzard Beach Water Park.

1 cup Patrón Silver Tequila
.5 cup Cointreau
.5 cup Ruby Red Grapefruit Juice
6 cups ice

Makes 4. Add tequila, Cointreau, grapefruit juice and ice into a blender and blend until smooth. Pour and serve immediately.

A Toast to Gary Carter

Gary Carter was a baseball catcher who was chosen 11 times for the All-Star team and was instrumental in the New York Mets 1986 World Series Win.
According to the *Merriam-Webster's Collegiate Dictionary,* Carter created the phrase "f-bomb" to describe the king of all swear words.
After retiring from baseball he coached college and minor league teams.
Visitors to EPCOT Center in the late 1980s might remember getting batting tips from a video version of Gary

Carter at Coaches Corner in Wonders of Life Pavilion. To a man who was taken from us too soon, Gary Carter!

Guy's notes: The Coaches Corner attraction also had two other coaches. For tennis it was Chris Evert and for golf it was Nancy Lopez.
The attraction worked a little like a Sega-CD game or a laser-disc video game (like Dragon's Lair.)
Several video responses were recorded with the athlete and then after the swing the computer would skip to a coaching tip that was based roughly on what mistakes you had in your swing.
Nearby was Wonder Cycles where you ride through Disneyland or other attractions that would be shown on a screen in front of you (along with your speed and calories burned.) The video accelerated and decelerated based on your pedaling.

Souse of the Future

Compare to 'Forever Young' at
The Wave... of American Flavors at
Disney's Contemporary Resort.

1 oz Tito's Handmade Vodka
1 oz Cedilla Açai Liqueur
.25 cup Muddled Blueberries
1 sugar cube
.5 oz Fresh Lemon Juice

Muddle blueberries and discard excess
pulp as desired. Add blueberries,
vodka and Cedilla Açai Liqueur into a
shaker with ice and shake vigorously
to properly mix blueberries. Strain
into rocks glass over ice and stir in
sugar cube until melted and add lemon
juice.

A Toast to Marvin Goody

Monsanto's House of the Future is one
of the most unique defunct Disneyland
attractions for two reasons. First, it
had a prime location. It was right at
the hub near Sleeping Beauty Castle.
Second, it was a house.
For ten years an all-plastic house

showcased video phones and microwave ovens right in the middle of Disneyland.
Marvin Goody was one of the architects of the house and he was a founder of

the architectural firm Goody Clancy. Today a memorial stands to him in the Boston Public Gardens and we remember him with this drink! To Marvin Goody!

Guy's notes: In addition to Mr. Goody, the design team included MIT professors Richard Hamilton and Albert G. H. Dietz as well as Frank J. Heger, Jr. and Frederick J. McGarry. The House of the Future saw over 20 million visitors over its decade of service.
There were rumors that after closing the house was airlifted to Texas where an eccentric millionaire lived in it. But the truth is that the house was demolished. Legend has it that they tried to demolish it with a wrecking ball, but the ball bounced off the plastic wall.

Sweet Home Coronado

Compare to 'Coronado Crush' at Siestas Cantina at Disney's Coronado Springs Resort.

1 oz Chambord Liqueur
1.5 oz Tequila
4 oz club soda
.25 cup muddled raspberries
1 sprig mint
1 lime slice

Fill glass halfway with ice and top with raspberries, add Chambord and tequila and stir in club soda. Top with mint and lime slice (floating, not on rim.)

A Toast to Benjamin Kine

Benjamin Kine was the vice president of the Tullytown, Pennsylvania school board back in 1954 when an unusual event took place. The students of the new elementary school were asked whom they wanted to name the school after. The students chose Walt Disney. Walt arranged to have original artwork adorn the school hallways and was on hand for the dedication in 1955.

Benjamin later secured the donation of an out of service Douglas D-558-2 Skyrocket to the school and kids were allowed to eat lunch in the cockpit. Let us toast to a fine man and to educators everywhere!

Guy's notes: This is a fun drink that is served at the Siestas Cantina which is an outdoor pool bar. It's just the perfect taste for cold day when you wish you were at some place tropical. The tequila delivers a good kick to this although the drink tastes even better with mezcal. Give it a try!

By the way, The Walt Disney Elementary School still has original Disney artwork and is now a designated National Historic Landmark.
The Skyrocket has moved on to the National Air and Space Museum in Washington D.C.

Swimming Pool Tee Hee

Compare to 'Poolside Iced Tea' at The Drop Off Pool Bar at Disney's Art of Animation Resort.

.5 oz Vodka
.5 oz Rum
.5 oz Gin
.5 oz Tequila
.5 oz Triple Sec
.5 oz Sweet-and-Sour
4 oz Coca-Cola®

Add all 5 liquors into a shaker and shake lightly. Pour cola into plastic cup one third full of ice. Slowly add liquors and pour the sweet-and-sour on top.

A Toast to Johnny Weissmuller In the 1930s swimming pools began to be used as marketing tools for large
American hotels. The Biltmore in Miami boasted the largest pool in the world and hired Weissmuller, an Olympic gold medalist, as a swim instructor. The handsome and fit

Weissmuller was a draw for the hotel and broke world records swimming at the pool until he moved on to Hollywood to become *Tarzan the Ape Man*. Weissmuller (as Tarzan) was represented by an animatronic figure in the Great movie ride! Cheers to Johnny Weissmuller!

Guy's notes: Like the Long Island Ice Tea, this contains no tea.
The Drop Off is a decent pool bar, but it is notably next to the largest pool on Disney property, The Big Blue Pool. This mammoth swimming hole houses 308,527 gallons of water. This means it would take over two million Swimming Pool Tee Hee cocktails to fill that pool! If The Drop Off ever gets a tour guide they can use that line for free.

This Shore Isn't Like Jersey

Compare to 'It's A Shore Thing' at Cape May Cafe at Disney's Beach Club Resort.

.5 glass prosecco
.5 glass Mango Popping Boba

This is easy, but weird and super fancy. Get out your finest white wine glass and spoon in the Mango Popping Boba until the halfway point. Then top with prosecco.

A Toast to Cornelius Jacobsen May

Disney themed the Boardwalk area to the New Jersey beaches of the past. Like Disney's version of Hollywood it's not precisely accurate, but rather the nostalgic version of the area people held onto in their memories.

The Cape May Café is named after the New Jersey city where the Delaware Bay meets the Atlantic Ocean.

Cape May (the city and county) are named after Cornelius Jacobsen May. A Dutch explorer and fur trader, May

explored and surveyed the Delaware Bay
on a ship called Blijde Boodschap,
which loosely translates to "Joyful
Message" so we send a joyful message
as we raise a glass to Cornelius
Jacobsen May!

Guy's notes: Mango Popping Boba is a
unique item out of Taiwan. These are
small mango flavored balls that look a
bit like caviar eggs. Not sure why
Disney chose these for a New Jersey
beach cocktail at one of their New
Jersey beach themed resorts, but it
sorta works!
The drink is light and refreshing and
the quirky look of the little orbs
reminds me of the sun, the sand and
beach balls all at the same time.
Disney uses sparkling wine (which is
just Champagne produced outside the
Champagne region of France,) but true
New Jerseyans would always choose the
Italian prosecco over anything French
or trying to be French. It's all
basically the same fizzy water. Drink
up!

To Kill A Duck

Compare to 'Tequila Daisy' at Dahlia Lounge at Disney's Coronado Springs Resort.

1 oz Don Julio Blanco Tequila
1 oz Torres Magdala Orange Liqueur
2 oz Grapefruit Juice
1 oz Lime juice
1 tbsp Hibiscus syrup
Splash of Soda Water

Stir ingredients (except soda water) in a mixing cup and then pour over ice into a cordial glass. Garnish with orange wheel.

A Toast to Sigmund Eisner

Sigmund was a manufacturer of clothing and the exclusive manufacturer of uniforms for the Boy Scouts of America. The Boy Scouts' distinctive uniforms are an iconic piece of pop culture and were parodied in numerous Disney cartoons from the 1938 *Good Scouts* (where Donald Duck acts as Scoutmaster on a hike with his nephews) to *Up* where Russel wears the uniform of the Wilderness Explorers.

It's possible that without Sigmund these iconic uniforms and these movie moments would still exist. However, Sigmund was also the great-grandfather of Michael Eisner, who was CEO of The

Walt Disney Company from 1984 to 2005. So without Sigmund there are many moments we would not have enjoyed. To Sigmund!

Guy's notes: Dahlia Lounge takes its name from the female character in *Destino*. This rooftop lounge has a décor that is also heavily inspired by this film. The view from the bar is very interesting. It's surprising to see how much green spaces there are at Walt Disney World.
The bar itself is a work of art with a surreal pattern of unique mirrors above it.

Datu of Mactan

Compare to 'Lapu Lapu' at Tambu Lounge at Disney's Polynesian Resort.

1 Pineapple (hallowed out)
2 oz Myers Rum
1.5 oz Orange Juice
3 oz Pineapple Juice
1 oz Sour Mix
1 oz LemonHart 151 floated on top

Mix the orange juice, pineapple juice and sour mix in a mixing cup. Fill pineapple with ice and pour in mixture.
Float LemonHart carefully on top.
Cover with pineapple top (with crown removed) and cut a hole to add a straw.
Peirce maraschino cherries with drink umbrella and stick on top for garnish.

A Toast to Lapu-Lapu

Disney fans love to order the Lapu Lapu cocktail, but few know the drink was named after the first Filipino hero. Lapu-Lapu, who had the title of Datu (or ruler) of the Mactan island.

Lapu-Lapu resisted imperial Spanish colonization in the 1500s and his name now graces an urban Mactan city, a national Philippine holiday as well as the Disney drink served in a hollowed out pineapple. It is with his spirit that we raise our mixed drink and say "Adlaw ni Lapu-Lapu!" ("Day of Lapu-Lapu!")

Guy's notes: This is a real Disney classic. Anyone that has ever visited the Polynesian Resort undoubtable saw someone drinking from a pineapple and immediately wanted one.
Disney uses Bacardi 151, but LemonHart is a much better choice if you can find it. Just make sure you are using a 151 rum. You want that potent rum floated on top.
To prepare the pineapple you need a pineapple corer. They are cheap and easy to find. Core that pineapple and save some juice for the cocktail… and eat that fresh pineapple!

Disneyland Resort

Disneyland Resort is the home of Walt Disney's original theme park. Walt famously told the story that he thought of the park because he was sitting on a bench, bored out of his skull watching his daughter's play on the merry-go-round. This isn't exactly true because Walt had been working on plans for an amusement park before he had children. Still, it's a good story. I guess we should just be thankful the cell phone wasn't invented yet. Then the story Walt would tell would be different. "And as I'd sit there on a bench while they rode the merry-go-round and did all these things, I played a whole lot of Candy Crush. That's why I opened a cell phone store in the mall."

Disneyland Resort is home to two parks (Disneyland and Disney California Adventure Park) as well as a Downtown Disney area and three Disney owned hotels.

Like the Magic Kingdom in Orlando, Disneyland Park avoided serving liquor until more recently. The hotels have always been a haven for travelers looking to bend an elbow.

There are some really fun things to see here, like the giant petrified tree that Walt claimed he gave as an anniversary present to his wife Lillian. Walt claimed Lillian didn't want it and they shipped it off to Frontierland. Of course, Lillian got even with Walt three years after his death when she married John Truyens and had the whole park renamed Truyensland.

Disneyland has been a place of great ingenuity since its opening. Even little things we take for granted, like the Disney trash cans.

Prior to Disneyland there weren't trash cans with an opening and closing flap. Most outdoor trash cans at that time were a wire mesh. They were unsightly and smelled. Walt Disney wanted something better and the Disney style trash can was created.

Next time you are tossing away the glass from a Disney cocktail think of

that innovation and tell yourself,
"Hey, I may be drinking garbage, but
I'm a Disney style trash can. I'm not
unsightly and smelly."

It's important to have positive
thoughts.

Now, on with the drinks of the
Disneyland Resort!

Departed Pateesa

Compare to 'Bloody Rancor' at Oga's Cantina at Disneyland Park.

1 oz Tito's Handmade Vodka
1 oz Ancho Reyes Chile Liqueur
4 oz Spicy Bloody Mary Mix

Mix ingredients and serve over ice in a goblet glass full of ice.

A Toast to Rod Warren

Rod Warren was a television writer who worked on several Christmas variety specials. He wrote Holiday themed musical shows for big names like Perry Como and The Osmond Family.
In 1978 he wrote for three different Holiday specials - *The Carpenters: A Christmas Portrait*, *Rockette: A Holiday Tribute to Radio City Music Hall* and *The Star Wars Holiday Special*.
The Star Wars Holiday Special is a truly weird special and stands out among stands out Star Wars and Holiday programs. Let's drink to Rod Warren and wish everyone a Happy Life Day!

Guy's notes: According to a 2016 *Star Wars* book, the Rancor in Return of the Jedi is named Pateesa.

Disney lays a candy "bone" across the top of the cocktail.
You can make these out of meringue.
Mix 6 egg whites and a cup of sugar and then shape your bones and put them on some foil in the oven at 200 degrees for 7 minutes.

You can find more detailed meringue recipes online. You can also find instructions to dance the merengue!
Then we can all dance the night away!

Whooo hooo! Happy Life Day, everyone!

Bloody Mimosa

Compare to 'Blood Orange Mimosa' at Hearthstone Lounge at Disney's Grand Californian Hotel & Spa.

2 oz Champagne
1 oz Solerno Blood Orange Liqueur
2 oz Orange Juice
splash of Grenadine

Fill champagne flute with 2 oz champagne and then add liqueur and orange juice. Add a splash of grenadine to give the drink color and garnish with a maraschino cherry.

A Toast to E. S. Babcock

Elisha Spurr Babcock was a businessman and tycoon who started his career in the railroad industry in the late 1800s. After he left the railroad industry he helped develop the Bell Telephone Company and owned the Eugene Ice Company. His travels took him to San Diego where, in March of 1887, he began construction on the elegant and magnificent Hotel del Coronado. The hotel was the single largest resort hotel in the world and has become a historic landmark and remains a popular destination. The iconic

structure was a huge influence on the look and style of The Grand Floridian Resort and (to a
lesser extent) the Disneyland Hotel at Disneyland Paris. For the beauty and recreation he gave the world, we raise a glass to E. S.!

Guy's notes: A 1992 L.A. Times article reported that the Hotel del Coronado put up a large inflatable mouse in front of the hotel wearing a shirt that said "Copy Mouse" (as a play on the term copycat... it took me a minute to get it.)
The article quotes Hotel del Coronado Chairman M. Larry Lawrence "It's all in good fun, if imitation is the sincerest form of flattery, the folks at Disney should be at least half as flattered as we have been in seeing that company's two replicas of the Hotel del Coronado."

Good Old Duke

Compare to '"The Duke" Old Fashioned' at Catal Restaurant at Downtown Disney District, Disneyland Resort.

2 oz Maker's Mark Bourbon
1 dash Fee brothers Orange bitters
1 dash Fee brothers Cherry bitters
.5 oz cherry juice
.5 oz orange juice

Mix your syrups and set aside for 30 minutes to settle. Add whiskey, bitters and juice to a rocks glass and add orange peel for garnish.

A Toast to Helen Aberson-Mayer

If you were to make a list of one-hit wonders in the world of children's books, Helen would make the list. Her sole hit was a mighty one. Helen wrote the story for *Dumbo the Flying Elephant* and sold it in 1939 to become a Roll-a-Book. This was a novelty toy where children could roll the pages of a book across a screen. Roll-a-Book then sold the story to Disney and Helen received about $1000.
Disney released Dumbo just two years later and film was a bit of a

departure since the previous feature
narrative films they made were based
on stories from the 1800s.
Helen wrote more children's books, but

none were published and have not
surfaced in the years since her death.
However, the one story she gave the
world was all magic. To the woman who
made us believe an elephant could fly!
To Helen!

Guy's notes: Interestingly no copies
of the Roll-a-Book version of Dumbo
have ever been found.
There is debate as to whether the
Roll-a-Book was actually sold at all.
Disney has purchased other books
outright before they ever were
published. *The Love Bug* is based on
based on the 1961 book *Car, Boy, Girl*
by Gordon Buford.
I went to multiple libraries looking
for this in the 1990s. Today it's
pretty clear that the book was never
published.

The Jekyll and Hyde

Compare to 'Hyde Old Fashioned' at Catal Restaurant at Downtown Disney District, Disneyland Resort.

2 oz James FC Hyde Sorgho Whiskey
2 dashes Orange bitters
.3 oz Amoretti Coconut Cream syrup
.3 oz Amoretti Dark Chocolate syrup
.3 oz Amoretti Vanilla syrup

Mix your syrups and set aside for 30 minutes to settle. Add whiskey, bitters and syrups to a rocks glass and add orange peel for garnish.

A Toast to Joan Crawford

Joan Crawford was a Hollywood star who made the transition from silent films to talkies, and starred in over 100 pictures. Today, many people first think of the "tell all" book *Mommie Dearest* that her daughter released after her death.

However, there are other interesting footnotes to the life of Joan Crawford, two that tie to Disney. First is that she was used as the inspiration for the look of The Evil Queen in *Snow White and the Seven*

Dwarfs and second that she is the force behind the existence of It's A Small World.
Less than a year before the 1964

World's Fair Pepsi was still trying to figure out what their sponsored UNICEF attraction would be. Joan suggested that Walt Disney be brought into the project and the result is a ride and an iconic song that appears around the world. Raise your glass to Joan!

Guy's notes: The name of the Disneyland cocktail comes from the James FC Hyde Whiskey, but I thought the juxtaposition of Joan Crawford's involvement in "The Happiest Cruise That Ever Sailed" yet having such a reported dark side seemed fitting that we call our drink Jekyll and Hyde.

Long Beach Mule

Compare to 'Anaheim Mule' at
California Grill at Disney's
Contemporary Resort.

1 oz Hangar 1 Mandarin Blossom Vodka
4 oz Ginger Beer
5 Splash of Orange Juice

Best with chilled vodka. Slowly pour
Ginger Beer into copper mug. Add the
vodka and splash of orange juice and 2
to 3 ice cubes. Garnish with orange
peel.

A Toast to Henry J. Kaiser

Henry John Kaiser is known as the
'father of modern American
shipbuilding.'
It was an odd partnership with
business magnate and pilot Howard
Hughes that has us honor him with a
toast.
In 1942 the United States needed to
transport materials and soldiers to
Britain. Henry's company was building
ships for the effort, but Henry
approached Howard Hughes with an idea
to create the largest aircraft ever
built.
The Hughes H-4 Hercules was nicknamed
Spruce Goose by the public, but was
actually mostly birch. The plane was

only flown in test flights and barely got off the ground.
In 1988 Disney acquired the plane and set out to create a destination called Port Disney. Like the Spruce Goose, Port Disney barely got off the ground. Still, for this odd bit of Disney history we salute Henry Kaiser!

Guy's notes: Disney calls this the "Anaheim Mule" playing off the name of the city where Disneyland is located. The difference between this and a traditional "Moscow Mule" is that this has orange juice instead of lime juice, which is a pleasant change.
This is likely done as a nod to the orange groves that once populated the land that today is Disneyland.
We named our version after the city of Long Beach which is the coastal community to the west of Disneyland.
It is the home to the Queen Mary and was once the home to Howard Hughes' Spruce Goose.
The copper mug really helps keep the drink cold, but if you don't have one use a Collins glass. Or if you're Howard Hughes, make a giant glass out of birch.

Tastes Like Emu

Compare to 'Smoked Turkey' at Steakhouse 55 at Disneyland Hotel.

1 oz Wild Turkey 101 Bourbon
1 oz Red Stag Black Cherry Bourbon
.3 oz Grenadine
2 oz Odwalla lemonade
Dash of Hickory Smoke
3 Maraschino Cherries

Mix all ingredients in a shaker and pour over ice in a rocks glass.

A Toast to William Strickland

William Strickland was an Englishman who sailed to the New World under Sebastian Cabot in the 1500s. He brought back American turkeys to England. The turkey became popular in England and when settlers started moving from England to America they continued to eat turkey. Of course, turkey was the featured dish at the first Thanksgiving in 1621.
Then in 1980 Disney began selling smoked turkey legs in Frontierland and the turkey finally cemented its place in history. So next time you're chomping on over a pound of turkey in the hot Orlando sun, think of William

Strickland who brought the world this delicious treat! To William!

Guy's notes: Disney garnishes with three Luxardo Gourmet maraschino cherries on a large toothpick laid across the top of the drink.
These are really great cherries and worth picking up.
Red Stag Black Cherry Bourbon is usually available in airplane bottles which is good if you are only looking to make one of these.
Red Stag Black Cherry does taste really good over ice so if you do like it it's worth getting a whole bottle.

The name refers to the absurd rumor that Disney sells Emu legs as turkey legs. Disney's enormous turkey legs are actually from Tom Turkeys (which can be up to 50 pounds.)
Emu is more expensive than turkey and it would be illegal for Disney to sell one type of meat and sell it as another. It's not illegal to call a drink "smoked turkey" however. Weird.

Vern's Daiquiri

Compare to 'Ernest's Daiquiri' at Carthay Circle Lounge at Disney California Adventure.

2 oz Bacardi Superior Rum
.5 oz Luxardo Maraschino Liqueur
.5 oz Fresh Lime
.5 oz Grapefruit Juice
1 tsp Agave Nectar

Shake ingredients vigorously in a shaker with ice. Make sure nectar has been thoroughly mixed. Strain and pour over ice.

A Toast to Jim Varney

Jim Varney was known to the entire world as the annoying - yet charming - Ernest P Worrell.

Jim played that character in a variety of commercials, movies and TV projects. Quite a few dealt directly with Disney parks. *Ernest Saves Christmas* was almost entirely filmed on WDW property and in the Orlando area. Vern's house was part of the

Disney-MGM Backlot tour for years. *Ernest Goes to Splash Mountain* was a 1989 TV special where Ernest was the first to ride the flume ride. The truest of EPCOT fans will recall Ernest's face from a gag in the pre-show for Cranium Command. For all this, and for giving a voice to Slinky Dog, we salute you, Ernest... er... Jim... Ah, you knowhutimean. To Jim Varney!

Guy's notes: The name of Disney's drink is a reference to Ernest Hemmingway who is attributed to having invented and/or popularized this version of the Daiquiri.

In Conclusion

Well, that's it. We learned some things, you and I. We had some fun. I hope you didn't try all of these in one sitting.

Making Disney cocktails at home can be a fun way to recreate the feeling you had when you were at Disney. I know it did for me.

In closing I want to misquote Carousel of Progress.

Remember how the grandma says "What will they think up next?"

Then Patricia says "Who knows? We've got a whole new century waiting for us out there."

Sarah chimes in with "Yeah, and maybe sometime in the new century, your father will learn how to talk to our oven."

Then Father cheekily replies "I want a divorce," and they all laugh at him as drinks blueberry schnapps out of the bottle until he can't see straight?

That's progress. Someday, everything's going to be so automated, you won't ever have to mix a drink again.

INDEX OF TOAST SUBJECTS

Roarty, Michael 126
Rothafel,Samuel L. 98
Schweitzer, Albert 24
Shepherd, Jean 46
Skillin, Simeon 58
Smith, Bubba 76
Sperber, Burton 44
Strickland, William 158
Takayanagi, Kenjiro 111
Varney, Jim 160
Wadewitz, Edward 68
Waldron, Veryl 86
Wallace, Oliver 56
Warren, Rod 148
Weissmuller, Johnny 136

INDEX OF LOCATIONS

DISNEY SPRINGS
D-Luxe 86
The Edison 102
Enzo's Hideaway 100
Raglan Road 90
Stargazers 96
STK 92, 94, 98
T Rex 88

EPCOT CENTER
Akershus Royal Banquet Hall 30, 36, 48
Chefs de France 32
Coral Reef Restaurant 44
Le Cellier Steakhouse 46
Takumi-Tei 40
Teppan Edo 34, 38,
Via Napoli Ristorante e Pizzeria 42

FOUR SEASONS RESORT
Capa 110

MAGIC KINGDOM
Jungle Navigation Co. LTD 24

POLYNESIAN RESORT
Tambu Lounge 142

PORT ORLEANS RESORT
Scat Club Club 112

SARATOGA SPRINGS
The Turf Club Lounge 128

SWAN AND DOLPHIN
Bluezoo 122

INDEX OF LIQUORS

Myers's Original Dark Rum 112, 142
Parrot Bay Coconut Rum 108

SPIRITS
Apricot Brandy 36
Aquavit 36, 48
Belle de Brillet Pear Brandy 102
Leroux Blackberry Brandy 124

TEQUILA
Tequila (well) 134, 136
Blanco Tequila 76
Don Julio Blanco Tequila 140
Herradura Reposado Tequila 120
Patrón Añejo Tequila 44
Patrón Silver Tequila 54, 130
Sauza Silver Tequila 80
Tanteo - Jalapeno Infused Tequila 110

VODKAS
Vodka (well) 136
Absolut Berri Açaí Vodka 68
Ciroc Pineapple Vodka 116
Deep Eddy Ruby Red Grapefruit Vodka 64
Grey Goose vodka 92
Grey Goose Cherry Noir Vodka 118
Haku Japanese Vodka 40
Hangar "1" Mandarin Blossom Vodka 156
Ketel One Citroen Vodka 94
Ketel One Vodka 78, 100
SKYY Infusions Blood Orange Vodka 96
SKYY Infusions Blueberry Vodka 122
SKYY Infusions Pineapple Vodka 96
Smirnoff Citrus Vodka 128
Stoli Vanil Vodka 64
Tito's Handmade Vodka 66, 132, 148
Vikingfjord Vodka 30, 48

WHISKEYS & BOURBONS
Bulleit Bourbon 90
Crown Apple Maple Whisky 46
Fireball Whisky 56
James FC Hyde Sorgho Whiskey 154

Knob Creek Bourbon 86
Maker's Mark Bourbon 152
Moonshine Whiskey 124
Red Stag Black Cherry Bourbon 158
Southern Comfort 68, 112
Wild Turkey 101 Bourbon 158
Woodford Reserve Bourbon 98, 102

WINES & WINE DERIVATIVE
Champagne 32, 150
Prosecco 92, 100, 138
Sake 34
Sweet vermouth 42, 98

INDEX OF DRINKS
(ORIGINAL TITLE)

Not Your Daddy's Manhattan 98
Ottawa Apple 46
Patrón Platinum Margarita 54
Pepper's Ghost 116
Poolside Iced Tea 136
The Preakness Cosmo 111
Prince of Norway 36
Raju 40
Rum Blossom 74
Smoked Bourbon Gelato Shake 86
Smoked Turkey 158
Southern Hurricane 95
The Stavanger 48
Tequila Daisy 140
Very Berry Lemonade 62
zooberry 122

INDEX OF DRINKS (NEW TITLE)

Printed in Great Britain
by Amazon